Barry Sheene
The Story So Far...

Paradise awaited me. The highest achievement in motorcycle racing was more than within sight; it was there for the taking.

The 500cc title is not just a garland of honour, a trophy of war, earned on the battlegrounds of Europe. With the action speaking much louder than any words, it's a supreme test of nerve, skill, fitness and bloody-minded determination.

I wanted that world title . . .

Barry Sheene
The Story So Far...

A STAR BOOK
published by
the Paperback Division of
W. H. ALLEN & Co. Ltd.

A Star Book
Published in 1977
by the Paperback Division of
W. H. Allen & Co. Ltd
A Howard and Wyndham Company
44, Hill Street, London W1X 8LB

Star edition reprinted 1977

First published in Great Britain by
Studio Publications (Ipswich) Ltd, 1976

Printed in Great Britain by Anchor Press Ltd,
Tiptree, Colchester, Essex

ISBN 0 352 30143 0

ACKNOWLEDGEMENTS:
Grateful thanks are due to the following for their help:
Eric Vargiolu (DPPI), Malcolm Carlin, Jim Greening,
Francois Beau, *Motorcycle Racing* magazine, *Motor Cycle
News*.

Edited by Ian Beacham (Editor of *Motorcycle Racing*
magazine)

Contents

Tributes	6
Foreword	8
Prologue	11
The early days	15
Just a working lad	33
This boy shows promise	44
The young professional	55
Agony all the way	74
Off into Europe	81
Machine to beat the world	98
The great bike disaster	121
Away from the noise	144
The greatest year	151
The dream comes true	165
What a life	185
Me and my bikes	210
Achievements	223

Tributes

'Barry Sheene has been one of the best things to happen to motorcycle racing. He has gained the sport tremendous publicity. Far from being a big head, he is a nice guy and I for one am pleased he won the world championship. On the track he is straight and fair; he wouldn't cut you up on a corner. I have only one complaint — he goes too fast!'

Mick Grant — *Team Kawasaki racer*

'He has contributed more to the sport than any other rider I have known. Barry Sheene's willingness to be available to the fans and to the Press at any time makes him so popular. He has a likeable approach and appears to want to put something back into the sport.'

John Brown — *Motor Cycle News Grand Prix reporter*

'We racing cameramen have a difficult enough time getting through the crowds to photograph the aces but Barry Sheene will go out of his way to help us. It's not a case of his using the media. He realises we have a job to do. His attitude can only be admired.'

Jim Greening — *International racing photographer*

'Barry Sheene has lifted motorcycling through his popularity and his image into a respectable and respected sport. His activities might not always go down too well with the average fan but he has definitely brought the sport to the attention of the man in the street . . . and that can't be a bad thing.'

Chris Carter — *BBC motorcycling correspondent*

'He's worked very hard for his success but I always hoped he would do well. He has been through a lot of pain and suffering and deserved to win the world championship. He has been a marvellous son to us and both Frank and I are so pleased for him.'

Iris Sheene — Barry Sheene's mother

Foreword

Ask Barry Sheene exactly why he chooses to race motorcycles at speeds bordering on the incredible and a puzzled expression will cover his face. He will insist it is not down to a love of speed or danger. He just likes competing on motorcycles. There is no other explanation. Money is certainly not the dangling carrot.

Yet question any of the thousands of spectators who have gone specially to a road race meeting merely to see this guy perform and the reason for their presence, they will say, is to witness the sheer spectacle of his riding. They want to see the speed and hear the amazing scream of a magnificently-developed two-stroke machine kicking out over one hundred brake horsepower. But they have also come to be attendants to the nightmarish dangers that Sheene dallies with by pushing a hunk of machinery around circuits with unbelievable bravado.

What is it about Sheene that has made him such a motorcycling natural? Why is his popularity so blatantly obvious? On the track he has proved he can conquer all; he has overcome the competition, the fear, the pain, even the heartaches. Away from the arena, he is the pin-up boy, the glamour kid from Cockneyland who has made good. He is more than just the biking hero of the young working classes; he is a larger-than-life sporting VIP who could well have been created for a Hollywood screen drama!

No other rider in road racing history can really match his public following. Geoff Duke? Mike Hailwood? Giacomo Agostini? Big in their own way but they offered no real public property identity. They stood apart from the people who made them into stars.

Sheene is touchable, agreeable, in tune with modern-day attitudes. Children can drool over him, teenagers can rave over him and the rest just enjoy him for what he is — a well-paid racer who has neatly slotted into the vacant spot the increasingly glamorous sport has supplied most of the gloss on the exterior of motorcycle road racing.

If there is a formula for the kind of success he has obtained in such a short period of time it must be a careful blend of hard work, an eye for the breaks in life and a pursuit of the thing that offers the most enjoyment.

Sheene is a crowd-puller. he is commercial and clever with it. But he has never strayed out of his depth. This personable charmer will talk to both peer and peasant and will feel it is not just part of his duties to communicate with the plebs. He enjoys it, like almost everything else he does in life.

Sheene is good for the game of racing, there is no doubting that. He is also good for those who earn all or part of their living from the sport. But as a person, what is the real Sheene like after the tinsel and glitter of race day has been swept away?

It's easy to explain. He is just the same bloke. He is approachable, interested, close to his family and is a fair dealer. He would never be made a BBC newscaster but that is no character deficiency. Yet he would dash across the road to save a cat from a dog, sympathise at someone else's misfortune and generally generate kindness and courtesy.

That description should not portray him as a shining white angel because he is not. He says what he feels and always feels what he says. So he is sincere but he is professional enough to speak the right words as and when appropriate.

Sheene is a lively character who prefers to get his kicks out of flirting with disaster, although he would emphasise that he has reduced the risk aspect of his job to a minimum. Watching him in action and appreciating what he does he does superbly well, one can only express admiration and incredulity at his performance. He is the complete craftsman at his art.

IAN BEACHAM

Prologue

Paradise awaited me. One day and, by rights, I would be world champion. The highest achievement in motorcycle racing was more than within sight; it was there for the taking.

The 500cc title is not just a garland of honour, a trophy of war, earned on the battlegrounds of Europe. With the action speaking much louder than any words, it's a supreme test of nerve, skill, fitness and bloody-minded determination.

Machinery has to be equally as precise.

The 500cc world championship series demands much from every rider yet provides real satisfaction for just one man — the overall winner. To be second or third after eight or nine exhausting rounds offers little joy. First place is the only place in which to finish.

I had never been first in this class of racing when it came to the final count-up of points. Come to that, I never been second or even third. Sixth had been my previous best.

For riders like Hailwood and Agostini, and maybe Read, the glory years came so regularly that I felt the magic of always being crowned champion must have worn a little thin over the years. From the other side of the fence, I watched all three as a kid and never ceased to marvel at the way they performed yet I often wondered whether it was all pleasure for them.

Now that I was almost in their exalted company as a world champion, I was discovering the experience to be just the same as most children feel on the morning of Christmas Day. Excited, aware that gloom can descend when the surprise is over but, above all, supremely happy.

But for me the dream was about to come true. There was merely the Swedish Grand Prix to win or, failing that, to finish well up in the order and hope that the only two other riders who had an outside chance of pinching the glory would cross the line behind me.

Confidence had never deserted me and the level of personal optimism that July weekend was extraordinarily high. I knew I could do it. Ability and stamina I had proved I had in abundance. It was now down to the bike. That was my sole concern. Would the Suzuki play up?

Would the two-stroke take me through twenty-eight laps? Time would tell. Was it pieced together properly after the crash at Snetterton at the meeting before? We would find out sooner or later.

The build-up atmosphere was neither tense nor charged with emotion. For me, the pre-race preparation was little different from any other Grand Prix and, if anything, the mood of everyone in the camp was relaxed.

When the final pickings are to be made at most major sporting occasions, excitement is usually heavy in the air, and if there is a Briton in at the decider, the moment is often swamped in euphoria. There was none of that. The four Grand Prix wins already to my name and an almost unshaking belief that I was destined to be the world's number one, if the bike did not misbehave, possibly neutralised the situation for me. Or it could have been that I felt I had no real need to be in Sweden. I know I would not have been at Anderstorp's circuit if it had not been necessary to tie up the loose ends of the title chase. It was apparent why Ago and company sometimes regarded racing as not so much a joyous pursuit but more a job of work.

Before that big race, I felt no worry. There was nothing to fear. And one of the people who could spoil my memorable day would not be racing.

When John Williams on another of the four-cylinder Suzuki GB 500cc machines crashed badly right in front of me on the second lap of the final practice session, it didn't dawn on me that my ride the next day would be easier without his challenge. John was a team-mate, a good rider who could give plenty a run for their money on his day and if I had fluffed all the remaining rounds, and he had done exceptionally well, he might have taken the title.

I was right on his tail as we cornered at 80 mph with hardly a millimetre of slick tyre connecting with the road. I wanted to see if there was any difference in machine performances. John turned on the power too quickly, spun his bike round and high-sided across the track. He fell directly in front of me and I was forced to stand my Suzuki right on its nose to stop in time.

I pointed my bike off the circuit, dumped it on the ground and rushed back to see how John was. The world championship was forgotten. Anxiety for his well-being was my only concern. He was in real trouble; as well as being unconscious, he was struggling to get his breath. By emptying his mouth of the dirt he had scooped up from the roadside verge and pulling out his tongue which was blocking his throat, I managed to ease his breathing. I removed his full-face helmet and straightened his neck before unzipping the top half of his leathers. The ambulance took an eternity to arrive and, up to the time of my first aid, the marshals were just standing around looking. Maybe they didn't know what course of action to take. I was no medical wizard but I was competent in the basics of trying to keep a guy alive.

As I helped him to be stretchered into the ambulance, it was obvious he would be sidelined for the following day's 500cc race. I was worried about his condition and my concentration was not helped by both my machines running sick when I returned to the paddock. By the end of that practice session I could finish no higher than fifteenth fastest and I was supposed to be the world champion designate! A place on the front row of the starting grid was still

13

mine, however, after my quick lap in the first day's training period.

So there it was. As long as the Italian youngster Marco Lucchinelli did not win the race, I was home and dry. But all racing thoughts were cast from my mind as I drove back to my hotel that evening. I dined with friends and contentedly washed down the Chateaubriand with some palatable white wine. I knew it would not be hot the next day so there was no reason to abstain from alcohol, although it amounted to barely half a bottle.

Quite often flamboyant newspaper writers describe sportsmen as having 'the longest night of their life' before a decisive event. Tossing and turning through to the daylight hours is often a feature of this pre-contest behaviour. It wasn't my pattern that night. I crashed into bed at one in the morning, made love to my girl friend and slept like a log through to ten-thirty the next day.

I awoke totally relaxed after munching my cheese and yoghourt Scandinavian breakfast, the only bother I had in the morning was untangling the confused reaction of my mother at home in England who had seen a Press report that stated it was me and not John Williams who had crashed.

So everything was ready for the final act in my racing drama. I wanted that world title. Not only for myself but for Suzuki who had never captured a big prize, for my parents and friends who stuck by me during the bad times, and, perhaps most of all, I wanted to win to silence all those people who had earlier written me off as either not being good enough or not being fit enough.

The matter just needed finally sorting out . . .

Those Early Days

No need to emphasise the point because just opening my mouth gives me away. Born in the Gray's Inn Road in Holborn just about in hearing distance of Bow Bells, I am an authentic Cockney — and proud of the fact.

When I was born, my father Frank rushed from the maternity hospital and phoned a friend to say: 'I've just been presented with the winner of the 1970 TT.'

All my relations said I was too pretty to be a boy but although I apparently looked the picture of health during my first five years, I was really a sickly child. Even though my mother Iris had been longing for a brother to my sister Margaret, she must have regretted the kind of boy she was presented with.

Sleep was never one of my attributes because I would scratch myself something wicked when laid down in my cot and mostly kept everyone else awake. I suffered from infantile eczema until I was two and that was followed by asthma which made me wheeze and puff on many occasions right through until I was a growing teenager.

But, like all parents, they took all the rough moments in their stride and my father was already promising me a 'big Norton' when I was only a week old.

Neither of my parents are true Londoners. Dad's got a nice Cockney rasp about him but he came originally from Hertfordshire although his parents were from Chelsea.

Dad was the keenest of amateur road racers. He began with sprint trials in 1938 and was fairly well up in the list at the end of each event. One of his fondest memories is the successful day he had at the now disused Brooklands circuit.

It was the last Bemsee meeting before the war at that famous track and apparently everyone wanted to ride there on the Campbell circuit. Dad won a cup from that meeting. I know for a fact he came second on a 247cc Excelsior in the flying kilometre at a speed of 76.61 mph because he still has the certificate proudly hanging up, all brown and dusty, in the workshop.

He re-started after the war on freaky bikes like the Douglas and would go to places such as Blandford, Oulton and, believe or not, the Isle of Man for the Manx. Frank was strictly a clubman's racer and he decided to pack in the riding around 1956. His argument was that he wanted to spare more time with Margaret and myself while we were kids. But mother says that he wasn't away from the tracks for long before he turned to the tuning side of racing.

I was brought up at the four-bedroomed flat that went with Frank's job as general maintenance man at the Royal College of Surgeons in Holborn. For forty years, he looked after the building and sorted out any problems that cropped up with such things as faulty central heating or general repair work. If any pieces of equipment like microscopes or X-ray machines needed seeing to, he was the man to fix it. I suppose surgeon's mechanic was a more fitting description of his work.

It was a busy medical college where hopeful young doctors would come to take their final examinations. Mum was employed there too, as housekeeper, which meant she had the responsibility of cooking hundreds of meals every week for visiting surgeons.

Grandad Alec looked after a farm in the 'sticks' where they bred animals for cancer research work. He did that for forty-six years and then, ironically, grandma Mary died of cancer. Frank was born on the farm and learned to ride motorcycles there.

Mum came from Bromley just on the outskirts of

London were her parents lived until they moved to Brighton when war broke out. Iris's dad was trained as a surgical instrument maker but he worked in a factory for some time during his later life.

Frank's only break from his job was during the war. He was deployed in the fire service for a while and then worked in a factory making radar parts. But motorbikes played a big part in his life because he was nearly always in his workshop in the evenings doing something connected with machines.

Sister Maggie was born in Brighton after mum was advised to move out of London because of the bombing dangers during the mid-Forties so it makes me the only real born-and-bred Cockney in the family.

We did have a slight racing tradition in the family. Dad's bit was on a small scale but his brother, Arthur, was something of an ace on the speedway tracks.

Uncle Arthur also did some road racing but he was well into speedway and one of his most notable achievements was riding in the first ever League speedway match for Coventry against White City. You can't keep the Sheenes away from bikes!

Plenty of heavies in that game Arthur always recalls. Even he became involved somehow because he was suspended for a couple of weeks for allegedly using an oversize engine. One of the star names of the day was breaking the rules in the same way too and he told Arthur they would both get away with it. He did but Arthur didn't.

As dad did not make the top flight in racing, he could have tried to turn me into something special as most fathers are keen to do with their sons following unsuccessful careers of their own. But there was never any time he pushed me to ride bikes. He let me lead my life as I wanted to although his motorcycling background and

17

spare-time preoccupation with two wheels obviously had a bearing on my interest in riding anything that would go fast.

I came into the world at five to nine on the Monday evening of September 11th, 1950. Five and a half years before, Maggie was born at exactly the same time of night — and on a Monday evening as well. Frank's timing was always good!

But although I did have those illnesses as a boy, it didn't prevent me from running round in my toddler days. Mum tells me my first mount was a three-wheeler trike which I would pedal like mad and go haring round the corners. Iris reckoned I would finish up with someone hooked up on the handlebars one day. She says I was one for speed.

Frank would often sit me on his bikes before I could hardly walk properly, so I'm told, and, by all accounts, I liked the sensation.

Getting the feel of them, Barry tries out the Matchless belonging to friends of his father.

Energy I had plenty of, but my asthma did restrict what I could do. Some days I would be really bad and had quite a problem getting my breath. The next day I was perfectly all right, and, just looking at me, no-one would think I had anything wrong with my health.

Any emotional upset would seem to bring on an asthma attack. When riders I knew were killed or badly injured I would go proper poorly.

School had almost the same effect on me. I hated school intensely and all it stood for and there may be something to be read into the fact that I shook off all traces of asthma when I left the classrooms for good at fifteen.

About the second time I had been to the Isle of Man for the TT, I nearly snuffed it. I must have been about five at the time and went down with a bad asthma attack.

We were staying at a neat, little guest house near the bottom of Bray Hill in Douglas. Dad would help the blokes out with bike preparation in the paddock and we would combine his work with a holiday. Well, the island being as it is, usually damp and often wet, the conditions brought on another Sheene deep wheeze.

The people at the guest house called for the doctor who took one look at me and rushed me to Noble's hospital for oxygen. My blue complexion wasn't too encouraging! Three days later they let me out and I was as right as rain watching the racing. But the Island weather is regarded as being bad for asthma sufferers. The Isle of Man is bad full stop. But that's another story.

Mother refused to take me there for years after that because the thought that I had nearly died stuck with her for so long. I didn't go back until I was about eleven.

But I was never a weedy, fragile-looking kid like some are with asthma. I was as tough as any youngster of my age living in that part of London and no-one ever tried to pick on me because of my health disadvantage. It stopped me from doing most school sports, naturally, as I couldn't get my breath to run but I wasn't unduly bothered. So I was about the most non-sporting boy you could care to meet. When I had my tonsils and adenoids out and my sinus scraped, it cut down the number of attacks but the inclination for active sport had gone forever.

I used to like swimming but that was about the limit. At my secondary school, St. Martins in the Fields, they used to go a bundle on football but I never reckoned that. And if I didn't play, I'd go down to the playing field and be caught for smoking and be sent back to school, more often than not, to get a caning.

For me school was like a bad dream. Every minute of every day was murder. I hated being told what to do and when to do it by a bunch of teachers who always wanted to try to insult and belittle me. I could do the subjects. No trouble. But I just couldn't be bothered to try hard. I knew I had it in me to do as well as any other kid but I just didn't have the interest.

Incredibly, the headmaster told my mother that my personality would get me almost anywhere in life and my brain was good enough to have made me top boy at school.

But when someone asked me would I or could I do a certain thing, then almost certainly I'd say yes. If they said do this or that, then I refused to do it. That was my nature which has remained almost unchanged since.

School was a drag from the word go and the day I finished was one of the happiest days of my life. I came home that day near to Christmas with my blazer and cap torn to shreds. Tradition meant that I had to let the other boys literally destroy my school uniform — and I really enjoyed seeing them do it.

I finally realised that there would be no more caning which I had suffered from term after term. Mischievous would be a kind description of my behaviour at school. Unruly would be better. But the strokes I'd get off some teachers whom I reckoned were no cleverer than me would often be the result of getting caught smoking. That punishment book was full of lines like: 'Sheene — smoking in toilets — six strokes.'

For someone unfortunate enough to have a serious chest complaint it seems odd that I should want to smoke. But long before I was a teenager, I was puffing my way through packets of fags, Woodbines or Park Drive, depending how much pocket money I had on me.

Iris and Frank didn't know I smoked until I was about eleven when they found three packets in the saddlebag of my bike. Dad had a mate called Ted who worked with him in his shed and after being found out, Frank asked him to hand me a couple of Woodbines and said: 'If you can smoke these two cigarettes, I'll let you smoke.' Well, by that time, I was almost a seasoned smoker and I just sat down and quietly puffed my way through them with no trouble at all.

There was no chance of them stopping me from smoking anyway but I was never encouraged. By the time I was twelve, I was offering my own cigarettes to mum and dad. Before that, they would never leave their cigarettes lying around because they knew the packet would contain fewer next time with me about the place. I wasn't proud in having to resort to nicking fags from mum's handbag.

But well before I got into bad habits like that and mixing with girls, I was riding around on a motorbike at five. It was a 50cc Ducati four stroke which had been given to my father as half a machine. He rebuilt it for me. Before I went off to school I'd be on that machine and loving every minute of riding around our backyard. The same thing would happen at night. It only had two gears and I would kick it from one gear to the other, without using the clutch.

I'd race home from school, get the thing started and off I'd go, round and round over the tarmac. I could shift too. With dad's tuning, I reckon it was doing 50 mph at times. The neighbours would complain like mad over the noise, quite often directly to the police. But the law just reckoned I was one less hooligan off the streets, so they didn't bother doing anything about it.

I wasn't shown how to ride the thing. It was handed to me and I was told: 'It's all yours. Now get on with it.' I must have fallen off about twenty times the first day I had it but I'd seen bikes being ridden before so I knew what should be done. Soon, I found out where the throttle and brakes were and quickly realised I didn't know where the clutch was. By the end of the first day, I had it all together and I was making that little Italian racing engine buzz.

My parents were happy because I had something to occupy myself with and I was away from the busy road traffic in the front of our home.

When I was eight I progressed to four wheels. A square-bodied Austin 10, with special conversions by dad for me to reach all the pedals, was a fine present for an eight-year old. I loved it. All my school chums would pile in it with me and we would do lap after lap of my backyard. It was like a little soapbox with wire wheels but I somehow managed to teach sister Margaret how to drive it. By the time I was ten she had passed her driving test! Dad bought the car for a fiver and sold it not long after for £20.

But by then I was what you might call an experienced biker. After the Ducati, dad brought a Triumph Tiger Cub off the racer Mick Boddice for me to ride. Whenever the family went to a race meeting, I'd take the Cub over the fields.

When I was still eight, we went off to Spain to see the famous Barcelona 24-hour race and dad became friendly with Francesco Bulto, chief of the Spanish Bultaco outfit. They had a new machine there which Senor Bulto allowed me to have a go on. Two mechanics had to stand either side of the machine to stop it after my fling because my legs didn't even reach the pedals.

Dad showed a big interest in one of the new Bultacos

and he later was able to acquire the first racer from them into Britain. Bultaco were to make the first major and significant contribution to my motorcycle racing career.

I was not an ordinary kid. Those games that a lot of schoolboys indulged in like marbles, cigarette card and stamp collecting were not for me. Wheelies on my push-bike and the occasional run-out on my skates was the nearest I got to being like the rest of my class-mates. Moving around with a gang or visiting the local youth club had no appeal. But I was trying to grow up fast and dad didn't help my ego when he caught me with several copies of 'Health and Efficiency'. 'Disgusting,' was his only comment, then he sat down to read them. It was motor-cycles that interested me most then and the real friends I had at the time were much older and tended to race bikes!

I had the Cub for some time and then, later, I rode a Bultaco Sherpa. Trying out my luck, I'd ride these

The mischievous
grin at eight years of
age.

machines around the block as often as I could. But I'd get caught now and again by the police who would give me nothing worse than a friendly warning. They didn't like to nick me because dad was in their good books. If ever the local cops had a prang in their patrol cars, they would come round to dad for him to repair them on the quiet so they didn't have to enter the fact about a crash on their reports. It was a case of, 'I'll scratch your back, if you scratch mine.'

When I was around eight, without him knowing, I got into dad's sparkling, almost new, Austin A50 which was parked outside our home and with a little girl Audrey Holman from down the road standing in front and telling me where to stop the vehicle I would release the brakes and show how clever I was at being able to 'drive' a real car. Dad almost had a fit when he came out.

My early years as a lad seem to be littered with pranks. Once I brought a boy home from school and encouraged him to drink a horrible concoction of spirits. Whisky, gin, you name it, he drank it. Drunk as a lord was a mild expression to apply in that case. He was completely gone when I took him back to school and it was decided to have his stomach pumped at the hospital. Another caning came my way and I think mum and dad got hauled over the coals for that from the headmaster although they were both in the Isle of Man at the time. I remember shuffling into the head's study, all clean and nicely carpeted, with dad flicking his cigarette ash everywhere. The head was hoping to get stricter parental control but all Frank would say was: 'Boys will be boys.'

But gradually, as my interest in bikes grew and grew, the rebel in me seemed to slowly fade away. I would still be against conforming but I was beginning to adopt a more mature approach to life, although I had lost little of my brashness. Dad and I would nearly always be at a race meeting every weekend and I was never slow in coming forward to tell a rider he had something wrong with his machine.

Looking back now, they must have thought: 'You cocky little bugger. What do you know about bikes?' But the fact was that I had a great understanding of most matters relating to motorcycles mainly because I had patiently watched my father take apart, mend and reassemble machines of all kinds. He had never carefully explained to me, bit by bit, what had to be done. It was a case of me looking over his shoulder and watching him put all his experience into action.

But some racers would tolerate me and I used to set up the carburation and float levels and stuff like that. On occasions, riders would suggest to their colleagues in trouble: 'Ask young Sheene, he'll help you out.'

I quite often rode racing bikes Frank had prepared for other riders on airstrips and around paddocks and generally got the feel for a machine. I knew when it was running rich or weak and it gradually became easier to realise when something wasn't right.

Frank's bikes were in a big demand in the mid-Sixties. Phil Read and Bill Ivy were just two star names who had great confidence in mounts prepared by dad. Dave Croxford was another. Dad always reckoned he rode AJS 7R's and BSA Gold Stars for fun before he packed up actively racing in the Fifties but he certainly took the mechanical preparation work very seriously.

Every time we went out, I'd watch the blokes on dad's bikes, note how they would handle them, listen for anything that sounded off-song. I certainly knew how an engine worked even then. While other lads would know who played outside-left for Arsenal, I could explain the principles of a two-stroke motor.

I used to have my own hero in those days. He was a chap called Denis Ainsworth. I don't know where he came from and can't even recall the kind of machine he rode. But I always remember him being a young guy who was always nice to me. He often said 'Hello' and would let me sit on his bikes. I hero-worshipped Bob McIntyre too at the time then but Denis won on points because he was young and I could relate to a bloke of his age more easily.

When I was ten, all the people who would come to my father to have their bikes done would say: 'I'm off to Brands on Wednesday for a spot of practice'. So I would always pipe up with: 'Can I come with you?' And usually I went.

The TT races were something of a highspot in my year as a lad. Dad would help blokes with setting up their bikes and I'd watch the boys from places like Governor's Bridge, the bottom of Bray Hill or somewhere up on the Mountain. Bob Mac used to go well there and I loved to see him flying down the roads. What a great sight.

But I never ever had thoughts of being a racer. I just didn't have any inclination to be one. I just sat back and enjoyed the races like all the other spectators. It never occurred to me or to anyone in our party that one day I would be one of the motorcycling big names.

All this talk of visits to the Isle of Man and to Spain plus racing excursions most weekends might suggest we were a relatively wealthy family.

We weren't well off, neither were we poor. I should say we were just a little bit above average for the simple reason dad had worked bloody hard. Once he'd finished his main job at the surgeon's college, he'd gulp down his tea and then work for hours fixing someone's car or bike to earn extra money.

With mum out at work too, it meant we could afford holidays in Spain and I went there from 1958 right through to 1966. We'd always combine the trip with a big race meeting, either at Barcelona or Zaragoza or Madrid.

The whole of my youth was motorcycle orientated and

there was only about one other interest that took my mind off two wheels. That was girls. I'd take out girls from school or else I'd go dancing on a Saturday night at the Empire in Leicester Square just down the road from home. I may have been only about fourteen but I could dance really well and had no difficulty in getting along with young ladies. At that age, I found out what it was all about over a snooker table in the crypt of a local church. Her name escapes me.

Drinking was never a weakness with me. I didn't touch the stuff until I was sixteen but I'll never forget my first taste of alcohol. It was in the Isle of Man in 1961 and the man who got me canned was Gary Hocking, the Rhodesian who was then a big MV Agusta star all over Europe. I was sitting by his knee talking to him and he kindly offered me two glasses of celebration champagne after he had finished second to Phil Read in the Junior TT on his MV and, in doing so, set up the fastest lap.

I drank the stuff like lemonade. Knocked it back like a fool and got pissed out of my brain. It taught me a lesson and maybe that was the reason why I steered clear of drink for five years after that.

Anyway, mother reckons I was a good, well-behaved lad and, for certain, I was never in trouble with the law. School was different and if she found out all the things I got up to, she would have died of shame.

Wednesday would be my favourite day of the week. More often than not, I would be a long way from those lines of dismal desks and ranting teachers who seemed so keen to try to make kids like me feel two inches tall.

That was the time of the week to head for Kent on the Southern Region trains. I'd get off at Swanley station and thumb it from then on to Brands Hatch. It was easy for me to skive off school without being found out. I used to have to attend an asthma clinic and, once, when I was there being examined I pocketed a whole stack of appointment cards that were already stamped and signed by the doctor. Boy, that was a marvellous find.

I'd fill in one of these cards with times like 10.30 am for the asthma clinic and then, on another one, put 2.15 in the afternoon for the bronchitis clinic. So that was my plan nearly every Wednesday — and I was never caught. There was no doubting the appointment by the teachers because they knew I was an asthma sufferer. I think I was a pretty shrewd operator because I would ask someone's father to write in the bogus appointment times so that my handwriting wouldn't give the game away. So off I went to Brands in my jeans and T-shirt, or Fred Perry shirt and bowling shoes, depending what the fashion was then.

But one day playing hookey a week was never enough and so it seemed like a good idea to take a month off school when I had the chance to go abroad as a mechanic to a racer — at the tender age of fourteen. My excuse to the headmaster was that I was ill and he seemed to believe me. There was nothing he could have done anyway as caning appeared to have no effect on my feelings towards the school and the educational system.

I'd been doing a bit of trials riding at times on my Bultaco Sherpa and there, I suppose, I just picked up the competition spirit.

The chance to go to the Austrian and West German Grands Prix came when Tony Woodman, an American, became a friend of the family after his mate Gerry McDonald had come to dad to sort out his Bultaco. By this time, dad was getting a reputation as the Bultaco king in this country and Bulto would send over two new machines every year for Frank to allow some rider to try out on the race tracks. It was really a way for Bultaco to spread the name of the marque around in this country and the factory knew that the bikes would be in reliable hands with Frank doing the preparation work.

28

Gerry returned to the United States and so Tony, who had a 500cc G50 Matchless and 350cc 7R AJS, was left on his own. He must have seen how handy I was with bikes but, if he was amazed at my mechanical knowledge, he never mentioned the fact.

My parents were great about it all. Although it was to be the first time I had been away without them, they knew I wasn't going to be silly or do something I'd later regret. It was a great experience. Pumped with excitement, I was being treated like a grown-up for the first time and I got on terrifically well with the lad from New Jersey.

He had complete faith in me. No arguments, no hassle. I would do things like changing the gearing, line the wheels up or alter the jets. Just average kind of mechanic's work.

Tony and I would sleep in the back of his Ford Thames van and have a brew-up on a little Primus stove in the morning. It was a real hippy-type existence but I thoroughly enjoyed it despite all the rough and readiness.

He was a talented rider, a bombshell from America who was shaking up the established track stars of Europe. If I remember rightly, he was leading this Austrian GP race at Salzburg by about a lap until he fell off in the rain at a cobblestone hairpin, and broke off the gear lever. In the German round, he made fourth place. There were no wages involved. I was just content to be considered good enough to be his mechanic and was not bothered about not being paid. I didn't want any money. It was a privilege just being there. Even the hunger pangs from frequent spells without food never over-worried me.

Frank had given me £15 to go away with for the month. That was to pay for my boat fares, a spot of occasional eating and for my cigarettes. But it covered all my needs.

There was I, a rather stringy boy, tinkering around with good machinery in the presence of the world's top riders. I thought if only my school teachers could have seen me. Veteran Swiss rider Guyla Marsovszky really tried to tease me and play me up in the paddock and so did a lot of others like the old Australian Jack Ahearn. But it was all in good fun and I didn't feel out of place. It was my first ever Grand Prix although, at the time, the importance of the occasion, the prestige of the event, failed to over-awe me.

When I returned to England, they reckoned I was a changed lad. I had grown in maturity and was head and shoulders above my class-mates when it came to experience of life. Mum and dad had written a sympathetic letter for me to take to school to explain my month's leave of absence and it seemed to work the trick. I think the school were glad I had been taken away because I was known to be such a hooligan. I was in the punishment book more times than any other kid at school, yet the stick didn't act as a deterrent to me.

They tried to make me eat school dinners. The teacher on duty would yell at me: 'You've got to eat!' So I would shout back: 'Well you make me then. You can stuff it in my mouth and shut my jaws tight, but I won't eat it. Even if you cane me I still won't eat it.'

What an aggravating so-and-so. The teacher would go almost purple under his collar and he'd scream at me: 'That's good food you're wasting there.' So back I'd come: 'You must be used to eating like a pig then.'

Then on other occasions, I would saunter into a lesson and that particular teacher on duty would say: 'It's a waste of time trying to teach you anything Sheene, just go to the back and read a book.'

So I hopped into the back row and opened up my *Motor Cycle News*. Another teacher in a different lesson would catch me reading *Motor Cycle* and confiscate my paper just as I was getting to an interesting bit. That enraged me, something like that, and it would make me storm out and go home.

I was a completely hopeless case. No wonder the school were glad to see the back of me when I was old enough to leave for good at fifteen. Of course, I hadn't a solitary exam qualification to my name and, on paper, I was a complete failure.

Bike made for two. Teenager Barry with his new Bultaco Sherpa trials machine.

Tony Woodman had gone to Northern Ireland with his brother but had crashed badly in the North-West 200 event and broken his back. That was a terrible thing to happen to such a nice fellow and the news that he was paralysed from the incident upset me almost as much as anything else that had happened before in my life.

He went back to America but later returned to England in the mid-Seventies and was a keen spectator at most major meetings, where we would meet and talk about past times.

But I had the future to think of. What would I do? Where would I go? Big decisions for youngsters to make at fifteen. I just let events happen.

Just a Working Lad

There was always enough pocket money. Mum and dad were good about something like that and I was hardly ever short of the cash if I wanted to buy a motorcycling magazine. A few more bob would come my way from the repair work I would help dad with in the evening. Our name as experts in the crash and tuning business had spread and there was a constant stream of customers into our workshop in the late Sixties.

But I had never experienced working for someone other than Frank and I wasn't quite sure how I would take to someone giving me orders. I had had a bellyful of teachers telling me what I ought to be doing but I realised I would not be able to adopt such a rebellious attitude to the new master who would be paying me.

To say the world lay at my feet whef I left school would be a lie. In fact, it would be more honest to say my prospects of landing a well-paid interesting job were practically non-existent. An 11-plus failure, a virtual secondary modern school drop-out with not one exam pass, put me at the end of the queue for the right jobs. Yet it never worried me one little bit. I knew I had a strong understanding of most things mechanical and I reckoned, as did my parents, that that would see me through into a secure position.

I wasn't sure what I did want to do. It certainly wasn't working in a car spares warehouse which I somehow got fixed up with when I was fifteen. There was nothing to be done all day long apart from listening to music on the radio. All I was required to do was to stick new spares in

33

different bins. Highly intelligent work. I was being paid £5 a week for working from eight in the morning until six during the week and from eight until one on a Saturday. Out of that princely sum came my National Insurance contribution and income tax.

So I would end up with around seventy-five shillings a week which was pretty awful, and that was only back in late 1965. It didn't go far with me. Needless to say, I had itchy feet and a vacancy for a lad to work for an advertising agency seemed fairly appealing.

Now that was a fantastic job. I was the sweet little boy who rode around London on a motorbike and did all sorts of things in offices and studios. It was enjoyable, even more so because there was a lot of crumpet around with different models coming and going every day.

I was out and about town all day long and my wage rocketed to £12 a week with a spanking BSA Bantam machine thrown in to go about my business. There was a nice lot of delectable twenty-five-year-old dollies there who would teasingly say to me: 'If you were a bit older, I'd fancy you.' To which I would reply: 'Well, I'm still big enough.'

Minding the Bultacos in Barcelona.

34

The Bantam was a real demon machine. I bombed about the centre of London on it and managed to break the gearbox four times. Frank tweaked the engine and it must have been knocking up 80 mph at times. I made that Bantam sing when I went off to deliver advertisement proofs for the agency.

By this time, I was old enough to be on the road legally, of course, and I had my own machine, a 75cc five-speed road-going Derbi which I took out on my sixteenth birthday. Failure to properly look after the bike made me fail my driving test on the thing. Little things began to rattle and fall off during the test, including the front number plate, and I knew I had had my chips long before the test was over. Although my Derbi wouldn't have won a Concours d'Elegance award, I passed my bike test the next time.

A friend came along one day and offered me even more money to work at his garage in central London preparing and smartening up secondhand cars for the showrooms and forecourt. Yes, I said I'd take it and I was there for eighteen months full-time. But I was then beginning to taste the delights of actually racing a bike and I needed time off in the week to see to the machines. So he gave me an ultimatum — either work or racing. I chose the bikes.

Yet, I realised I needed money to race and so it meant getting something on a casual basis that would fit in nicely with my racing schedules. Lorry driving sounded the ideal position for me and it happend that I knew of a vacancy that had cropped up.

The only problem was that applicants had to be twenty-one. As I was seventeen, I had to think fast. Finally I came up with the idea of showing the employer dad's driving licence, pretending it was mine. Anyway, they believed me and I was given the task of driving a thirty-eight foot articulated lorry around London. The loads were precious consignments of antique furniture. There was no such things as log sheets in those days, if there were I didn't know anything about them. It meant that I could put in all the hours I wanted to.

Handling a wagon that size presented no problem. I had learned to drive a car in Spain when we went on holiday. At fifteen, I was borrowing father's Rover 105 and taking a car-full of lads up the road to Sitges which was about thirty miles from where we were staying. When I was seventeen Dad had an old Thames van which he passed on to me for my personal use but it wasn't too flash for pussy-pulling. Later my car driving test was taken and passed in the Rover with no bother at all, when I was seventeen.

I knew how to look after myself then. I was growing taller all the time and coming from that part of London made you aware that there was no place for weaklings. One day at Brands I was sitting in the back of the van in the paddock and I saw a guy who had owed my dad some money for about three years. Dad had done some repairs on his racing bike and he had obligingly given him six months to pay the bill. But three years had gone by and still he wouldn't pay.

I rushed over and brought him to where Frank was. I asked: 'Didn't you promise to pay my dad that money?'

He replied: 'Maybe I did, but it's just hard luck. I won't be in a position to pay.' He insisted he wouldn't pay and dad would have been prepared to just write off the debt. I wasn't.

So I whacked him in the face and knocked three of his teeth out. He needed some stitches too. There was about £100 involved but it was more of the principle that I was concerned with. He was taking my dad and family for a ride, that was the reason. I was seventeen then and there was to be only one other occasion when I was involved in a flare-up like that again.

My height had increased quite substantially upon starting work and from the skinny youth four inches growth in a year made me into a fairly tall young man. My blonde streak in my hair on the right-hand side of my head was beginning to attract attention then. Tinting and streaking of men's hair became quite the vogue in the Seventies in London, but it took a lot of explaining by me to assure jokers then that I was not turning into a pouffo.

A couple of months before I was born, mum had a severe fright when a child stepped out into the road in front of the car her and Frank were in near home. Apparently, the shock, according to the gynaecologist, caused a birthmark on my head and since then it had always sprouted much lighter hair than my normal dark brownish crop.

But I digress. Already I was a proper racer. That's what I thought. Getting on towards eighteen I had finally made the breakthrough. Instead of watching and willing others to do well, I was now in the driving seat.

It was never a case of fulfilling a burning ambition. The pull of actually racing was never strong in those days. Contentment for me was simply to make ready or put right interesting motorcycles.

It would have been natural to start racing on one of dad's specials but it was to be Bultaco — a marque close to Frank's heart — that was to put me on the way to what was really the unknown. Nothing was expected of me then and I had little to lose by competing.

The chance came after Frank had 'volunteered' me to run-in a pair of Bultacos just received as the annual consignment from Senor Bulto in Barcelona. A week before I had found out what life was really like on the other side of the safety fences by taking out a little 50cc Derbi on the Brands circuit. Didn't rate the experience much especially as everyone was overtaking me. First time, too, that I had worn proper racing leathers.

Anyway, I thought I would see how dad's Bultacos would go even though I was only there for the motors to be gently run in. They must have performed well because it was the first time dad had not had a new Bultaco seize on him.

When I pulled into the pits at the end of the day's session at Brands, I had to admit it was a pleasant way to spend an afternoon. Everything had gone so smoothly that Frank felt I should have another bash running them in the following week. This time reports came through to dad that I was looking a bit sharp, a little bit nifty, on the 125cc and 250cc bikes.

All those guys who rang up my father to tell him how good I looked gave my confidence a massive boost and, amid all the head-swelling and excitement, we decided to have a stab at a proper race the next weekend.

Well, what a carry on. First time out on the 125cc Bultaco, I had somehow charged through the field to nab second place. As I was about to sail through what was then Kidney Bend at Brands, it all locked up and I was propelled over the handlebars. That's a seizure, I said to myself, as I bounced onto the road. It was something completely foreign to me, not having had one before. The cause was a needle bearing on the small end breaking up. I was banged about the head, cut my lip and lost some skin off my hands, but certainly wasn't bad enough to warrant the attention of St. John Ambulance officials and meat wagon into which I was gently eased.

But the only thing on my mind was the fact that I was down to take out the 250cc Bultaco in a race shortly to come. Dad was not sure. Coming off in my first ever race didn't do much for his nerves and, white-faced and looking worried, he seemed more shaken up than I was.

I wouldn't be put off though by his anxiety. He wanted me to scratch from the race but I was keen to show what I could do out there. Third was to be my placing and it might have been higher if I had not been just a little over-cautious about falling to another seizure.

I was feeling quite chuffed with my efforts that day and whenever I think back, I do reckon it was good going for a bloke with no racing experience behind him. Now so many people know about this first race — first crash business, because it has seemed to be mentioned in all major articles on me.

In that type of competition the Bultacos were good bikes to be on. Maybe some people expected I would naturally do well on gleaming new machinery that had virtually come straight from the factory but I was still a complete novice and getting the machine on the right racing line I found tricky at times.

But it was an encouraging start. The crash didn't do anything to dampen my enthusiasm. In fact I put the incident completely out of my mind by the next day. Dad was happy to let me have another try-out the next weekend, again at Brands. I couldn't wait for the next meeting to start, such was my excitement to improve on my last performances.

Again, I was down for two rides on Bultacos. The first race was a doddle for me and I couldn't believe I beat everyone to the chequered flag by twelve seconds. Oh boy, was I over the moon. I felt ten feet tall when I returned to the paddock. The feeling was hard to describe. I was shaking with excitement, there was a big grin right across my face and dad looked as elated as I did.

The next outing of the afternoon was on a rather extraordinary 280cc Bultaco which was, in essence, a bored-out 250 adapted with special piston. Dave Croxford was the rider earmarked to give it a whirl but dad thought he would use me as the guinea pig to see how it went in the 350cc race.

Trick bike or not, it went like a bird and I came home half a lap ahead of them all. Two wins in two races in only my second meeting was good going in anyone's language and I'll always remember one or two racers coming round to talk to me in the paddock after my second victory. When a couple of reporters from the motorcycling Press wanted to know how I achieved all that, I began to appreciate that winning could be very enjoyable. Just competing would have been sufficient for me although I must admit I was determined to do well once I was out on the start line.

But for all the knowledge I had stored up, it was a relatively late age to have my first dice on a race track. If I started a couple of years earlier — I could easily have fiddled my papers — I might have been British champion by the time I was eighteen. Thoughts like that did flash across my mind during the after-glow of the Brands success but a few days away from the action made me realise that I was still a new boy with so much to learn. That year Bill Ivy was killed while practising for the East German Grand Prix and I was so cut up. I had talked to Bill lots of times and loved to see him race.

I wasn't entirely sure regular racing was for me. To help dad out with his bikes was one thing, battling for honours at frightening speeds was another. A lot of thinking went into my decision to drop racing for a while in favour of taking up an offer, in April 1968, from Lewis Young who wanted a young mechanic to accompany him on the Grands Prix.

Lewis had Bultacos about which I knew nearly all there was to know and I felt the experience of tripping around the different European circuits, seeing quality riders perform, would do me more good than merely trying to improve on infrequent rides at short tracks like Brands.

Off we went to Sweden, Finland and then down to Germany, Holland and all points west. Lewis was well up in the ability stakes but it was the first time he had seriously ridden 125cc and 250cc Bultacos which he obtained straight from the works in Spain. In fact, I think it was the first occasion he had ridden a two-stroke. He certainly was lost if someone asked him about the motors.

The arrangement was more or less the same as with Tony Woodman. Nights were often spent curled up in sleeping bags in the back of a Thames van and, again, feeding times were few and far between. Nevertheless, it was bloody good fun. I learned a lot, made a great deal of acquaintances and the whole exercise I'm sure did a lot to lay the foundations for a racing career.

Talking of friendships, once before the Finnish Grand Prix I managed to bring a bird back to my room in the hostel we were staying in and, afterwards, when she wanted to go back home, Lewis refused to let me use the van. So I had to trudge four miles to her village and four miles back in driving snow. I didn't say much to Lewis the next day but I knew he was right not to let a teenager, keen to impress a girl, take out his vital racing transport on slippery roads at four in the morning.

But Lewis and I got on well all the time. Living so close in the most exacting of circumstances, you have to have an

On the 282cc Bultaco, Barry tucks himself in on another successful ride.

easy-going relationship. There were problems with the Bultacos, mishaps like the primary chain flying off when he would be well up in a race. Almost every other rider on a Bultaco was being plagued with the same trouble but at least I did manage to sort it all out by modifying the clutch. That was the end of broken chains and we were all chuffed that I pin-pointed the trouble-spot.

Seeing new countries and the way other people lived and reacted, convinced me I had made the right choice to go with Lewis. There would be plenty of other opportunities to race in Britain in the future but Continental trips were harder to come by.

The work would often be long and hard but I had no complaints. Even if Lewis was relaxing in another competitor's caravan, I didn't mind poring over his bikes till the small hours of the morning. I could never call it work, it was more of a hobby for me. Naturally, I took it all very seriously and I was always determined to ensure everything was just spot-on with the machines.

We returned to England in the autumn. I was twenty pounds lighter due to abnormal eating habits but fit in mind and body. Lewis stopped racing for a while, then went off to race in South Africa and the last I heard about him was that he had his own transport company somewhere near London.

Just occasionally during my stay on the Continent I had wished I had been the one pulling on the helmet and leathers to go out racing instead of standing there by the trackside, spanners in hand and spark plugs protruding from all pockets.

The prospect of competing again excited me when I came back and I knew in my heart that I could do better than some of the blokes I had seen touring around in the Grands Prix.

Lewis had left me his 250cc Bultaco which dad and I converted to a 280cc to contest the 350cc class events. With the two existing Bultacos that meant I had three bikes to enter the 125cc, 250cc and 350cc races which was a damn good set-up for a lad barely turned eighteen. Dad was still receiving the two bikes every year from Bultaco via the concessionaires Rickmans partly as a gesture of thanks for all the publicity he was getting the factory in this country.

I was ready to go!

An unusual trophy for his 1970 Spanish international race victory.

This Boy Shows Promise

Plans were made early in 1969 for me to have a regular programme of races throughout the season. I was looking forward to the competition and to racing on certain circuits I had never ever seen before like Castle Combe and Croft.

This was to be my first assault! Titles and trophies were waiting to be won. But it has to be said that I was not that ambitious at the time. The fun aspect of the sport took priority as far as I was concerned. If I won, all well and good, but if I was beaten — and there would be plenty of quiet days — I didn't let my spirits sink.

With every race, I was getting better as a rider, there was no doubt about it. People were beginning to sit up and take notice and there were moments when I was really confident I could win the 125cc British Championship. The standard of opposition was good then — there were people I couldn't beat!

Chas Mortimer was then the ace rider in that particular class and he was often showing me the way round. I was even beginning to get a few mini-headlines which read 'New boy makes good' or 'Sheene wins on debut ride'. But I was still largely feeling my way round on circuits that were completely strange to me. Going up to places like Croft was an experience in itself, chugging all those miles up the A1 in my beat-up Thames van.

Although I finished second to Mortimer in the final Championship classification, I was more delighted at being called the most impressive newcomer of the season.

It all helped to get more works backing from Bultaco which I welcomed.

Gradually it filtered through to me that there was some useful pickings to be obtained from the sport. Good sponsorship was the aim of any up-and-coming rider; Bultaco were helping out to a small extent and there was some assistance from various other tyre and spark plug concerns.

The Donald Duck motif on my helmet was now being seen around the tracks. I chose that unusual sign for my crash-hat because I reckoned it was so way-out that a lot of folks would have to have a second look and I was positive no other rider had displayed such a comical picture on a helmet before.

I was also to become the first rider ever to have his name on the back of his helmet. I was the one to start the trend and, since, hundreds of others have followed suit. It wasn't intentional. My helmet had gone away to a chap I knew to be painted, mostly in black, and it came back with my name emblazoned on the rear. That's neat, I thought, and I know I turned many heads when I unveiled it for the first time.

With so many promising-looking riders coming through the ranks at the end of the Sixties, it helped to be noticed if there were sponsorship rewards going. The best way I knew to get recognition was blow them all off on the tracks, and in 1970, I took in as many meetings as was humanly possible.

My chunk of luck for the early part of the season came in the form of Gerald Brown who was doing so much to help young racers. Sponsors like him are worth their weight in gold and for sure the sport does not truly give the credit men like him deserve for pumping in so much cash and expertise for practically no return other than the satisfaction of seeing their raceware perform well.

Gerald, who's from Cheshire, supplied me with a quick

250cc Yamaha motor to slot in one of our Bultaco frames. The 250cc Spanish wasn't as competitive as it should have been so the switch to the Japanese engine was considered the right thing to do. The move paid off in the opening meeting at Mallory Park in '70 where I won both 125cc and 250cc events and even managed to win a 500cc heat on a converted 326cc Bultaco. Needless to say, I was left behind when it came to the 500cc final which was packed with much more powerful bikes.

In those days, I had admiration for Dave Croxford, a respect which I have never lost. He always seemed to go fast and it never seemed to bother him if he crashed which he did quite a lot. He was always willing to pass on tips. But I considered it an honour to be asked to partner Dave in the annual 500-mile production race at Thruxton that year. We were out on a 500cc Kawasaki and Dave had excelled himself by keeping aboard the machine and even building up a good lead for our class. The day was ruined, however, by me. This was about the first time I had raced a big-capacity machine and my inexperience was perhaps responsible for me toppling off which put us out of the race.

The larger bikes did hold a certain fascination for me and I welcomed the opportunity to have another bash on one the following weekend at Brands. This time it was a 750cc Kuhn Seeley twin and I came in seventh. I suppose that was may first taste of superbike racing.

My trusty 125cc Bultaco was doing me proud and I remember being top of the British Championship when the second biggest slice of luck came my way.

Through the many contacts our family had built up in the racing game, we quickly heard that something special was going to become available. This machine was going to almost transform my career, pitch me into the big-time and generally help to make me a racing star.

Stuart Graham was selling his 125cc ex-works Suzuki twin and we realised that a lot of others would be interested in getting their hands on it. Stuart was getting rid of it because he decided to retire from racing for good. He hadn't taken part in many races for the two years before and he finally made up his mind at the TT.

The bike was going for £2,000 which was a lot of money in those days. It's still one hell of a figure to pay for a six-year-old secondhand machine that had been flogged almost to death even by today's standards.

But we knew what it had achieved in the past and what it was capable of. Although this Suzuki has been raced and raced, it was still a good machine, beautifully made and built to last for years.

I had to have that bike whatever debt I would get myself landed with. The bike was really pricey, there's no getting away from that, but it would win its races by a mile against strong opposition if ridden properly, and it had to be worth every penny.

In fact, it took virtually every penny I had safely stored away in my Post Office savings book. The lot went and, of course, dad loaned me a huge chunk of the money which brought his bank balance down to almost nil. That was a super thing for him to do because he had carefully tucked away any spare cash he had from his weekly wages to put to the nest-egg he and Iris would want for their retirement. But what confidence in me he must have had. I could have smashed the thing up against a barrier first time out and we'd have been left with nothing.

Luckily, nothing like that happened and our speculation over such a chancey thing as a racing motorcycle was to pay handsome dividends.

Let it be said, though, that everything dad gave me to make up the £2,000 I paid back. I was still doing the lorry driving and there were one or two odd-jobs that pulled in more money, things like shifting wood around in a timber yard, parking cars in a central London car park and fitting stereos in bloke's vehicles.

A whole stack of people reckoned I had Father Christmas for a dad, insisting that he bought the bike for his son. That's just merely jealousy. They'd say: 'His old man's got a lot of money. He'll finance Sheene all the way to the top.' Load of cobblers, that's all it was with them. They knew I had a fantastic bike and I was going to go places on it. Examples of sour grapes happen all the time in racing.

It was the best move I could have made. I was then super-competitive and able to out-pace most of my rivals in this country and many of them abroad. For sure, I would have never entered the world championships on my Bultaco in the 125cc class and I would have almost certainly stuck to the same level of competition for years without getting any better.

The ten-speed 125cc Suzuki would make all races in its class a virtual walk-over in England but it wasn't as fast as the Derbi or Morbidelli machines that were a feature of small-bike races abroad.

I picked up the bike on the Friday and raced it at Mallory for the first time in the Post-TT meeting on the Sunday but because of oiling plug problems I had only been able to get in five laps of practice on it. That was no time at all to find out the bike's quirks and habits.

It was so different from the Bultaco that, initially, I didn't think I was going to master the machine before I had the first real fling.

A quick glance around on the starting grid gave me the jitters. All the stars were there, men like Dave Simmonds then world champion, the West German ace Dieter Braun. It was a class field befitting an international meeting.

The first time for everything is always a funny experience. If everything goes well, the future looks rosy. An indifferent start and doubt and uncertainty creep in. Like

48

taking a girl out for the first time, I suppose.

My blind date was with a proven 100 mph machine. Now it was up to me to show we could live happily together. I started reasonably well but Simmonds buzzed past me. So I tucked in behind his works Kawasaki and figured out my next move. Gradually I was getting the hang of the Suzuki and my plan was to take Dave three laps from home. The plot went just right and as I hurtled out of Devil's Elbow towards the finish flag, I could hardly contain my delight.

From then on the Suzy and I struck up a good understanding between ourselves and we became just about the untouchables in Britain. It was too easy, to be truthful, and I paid heed to something some chap once said to me. He insisted: 'You don't want to stay in races you know you can win. You always want to contest the more difficult ones.' So that's what I eventually did at the end of 1970 and I never seemed to look back after making the decision to move up to international meetings. The move must have helped me no end because when I came back from abroad in 1971 to compete in international meetings in Britain, I would win the 125cc races nearly every time.

The first big honour: the Castrol Challenge Trophy for winning the 125cc British Championship in 1970. With his parents, Iris and Frank, is girl-friend at the time Lesley Shepherd.

In ordinary national meetings in this country, the Suzuki would be left at home because it was no match, no contest. Instead I would ride the Bultaco alongside all the other single-cylinder bikes, which were mostly Yamahas, and the racing would be that much closer.

That's not meant to sound conceited, I was just being plain level-headed. Who would want to see me tear around on the Suzuki with the rest of the field a lap behind? There was nothing to gain by doing that.

The 125cc British Championship — and £200 of Castrol prize money — was finally clinched at Cadwell where I won a close race from Cliff Carr but I was hoping for richer rewards than that from racing.

For me, there seemed only one level of competition I really wanted to ride in — and that was at world championship class. No point in leaving it too late I reckoned so I chanced my arm in the final round of the 1970 125cc series in Spain, a country where I had enjoyed many pleasant visits in the past.

The shock in some quarters that I was brazen enough to try my luck in the highest standard of racing after less than two full seasons in Britain was understandable. But you've got to keep moving on if you want to get somewhere in racing so I considered there was no time like the present.

By this time, I had teamed up with Don Mackay, my mechanic, who's twelve years my senior. We had known one another since about 1968 when Don used to bring a 250cc Bultaco over to Frank for him to prepare, and he gradually became a friend of the family.

It sounds incredible but it's apparently true, Don was a sponsor then. He put his money into supplying bikes for a guy he was friendly with called Gary Petken, but the chap chose to quit racing and so Don was at a bit of a loose end until he started up with me. That was another piece of good fortune for me because Don has worked wonders on my machines. His father came from the wilds of Scotland but he's another Londoner, from Kensington, and we seem to share the same zany sense of humour; needless to say we have always got on like a house on fire and he was happy to give up his job as an electrician to accompany me on my racing expeditions abroad.

Don's a bachelor, cheerful nearly all the time and is always anxious that the bike's just right. Funny thing about Don is that he hates the countryside and can't wait to get back to the streets of London after a race meeting.

While in Spain a week before my world championship debut, we decided to have a go in a big open meeting sponsored by Jerez, the makers of the famous sherry. Much to the astonishment of the partisan home crowd lining the track by the Mediterranean coast, I won the 125cc race on my ten-gear Suzuki and beat the local hero Angel Nieto on his works Derbi.

Now Derbi weren't too pleased about that and they redoubled their efforts to make sure the same thing didn't happen a week later in the final round of the classics.

Most of the crowd had come expecting to see Nieto thrash the opposition out of sight on the Montjuich circuit in Barcelona as he consolidated his undisputed leadership at the top of the championship table. The name Sheene meant practically nothing to them.

Well, I had a shock for Angel. In practice I was only half a second down on him and I'd never ridden the circuit before! My Suzuki had to have a six-speed gearbox in place of the ten under FIM rules and Don and I put in a Dutch-made box.

My gearing wasn't quite right, though, even though I was leading the race for five laps towards the end. I had to keep shutting off the motor when it got to 14,000 rpm on the fastest parts and had it not been undergeared, I'm sure I would have won.

Little Angel got ahead of me and he went on to win by eight seconds. But I managed to finish behind him 40 seconds in front of the next rider, Bo Jansson, who was a seasoned Grand Prix regular.

For some stupid reason, Derbi reckoned I was racing with the ten-speed box and although an official FIM investigation discovered it was only a six-speeder, I would have thought it would have sounded pretty obvious how many gears I had on the bike. They possibly just wanted to cause some aggravation after I had shown in two meetings that their star man was far from being unbeatable. Angel and I first met that year and we slowly built up a nice friendship which helped me with my command of the Spanish language. Now I can speak it fluently.

Even to this day, I don't think I have made one enemy in racing, certainly not among the people I know. There may be people outside my direct circle of friends, associates and acquaintances who want to do me down. I should imagine there are quite a few members of the public who feel the same. Whenever a sportsman or entertainer or whatever attracts popularity, there will always be someone who will resent that celebrity for his fame. It's a fact of life.

But Angel bore me no malice. He's a professional road racer who is only too well aware that every year will throw up someone to dispute his superiority.

At the same GP, I decided to race in the 500cc class. My practice times were incredible . . . even for me. I wheeled out my 360cc single-cylinder Bultaco as the mighty 'MV' fire-engines went howling past. If anyone was a no-hoper it should have been me. I could have been a typical holiday racer like you get in the Isle of Man TT. But what a surprise I had in store for everyone, including myself. I finished the practice session just a tenth of a second slower than the Italian Angelo Bergamonti on the 500cc MV Agusta. Although I had to retire from the actual 500cc race when the Bultaco seized I was up to second place at the time and was feeling cool and confident.

The whole Grand Prix scene looked just fine to me now I

was in the ranks of the riders and I was glad I had definitely decided to go Continental the following year.

Before leaving Spain, I took in a round-the-houses meeting at Zaragoza to try to make a few bob to help pay off my expenses. In good old British style weather, it chucked it down with rain all the time and they tell me it was the slowest road race ever run in Spain, if not in the world. The roads were like glass, one burst on the throttle and you were off, so I didn't intend to crash. Bo Jansson won the 125cc race on his Maico at an average race speed of 46.06 mph. I came second. I reckon push bikes could have gone faster than us.

Most of my association with racing motorcycles had been with the smaller type of bike. But it didn't stop me from thinking I'd like a good crack at the 500s and 750s one day. The chance came earlier than I thought possible. Suzuki GB's works 500, or what there was left of it, became available after the 1970 Ulster Grand Prix. Malcolm Uphill had a terrible crash on it and badly hurt himself. I think dad and I spent only about £40 on it putting it near enough right and, after adding a Seeley frame, it must have ranked as the bargain of the year.

My first attempt to race it came at Snetterton but although I was able to squeeze some good lap times out of it I finished out of the prizes in the final.

At the end of the season I had clinched the 125cc ACU title and was third in the 250cc British Championship behind Steve Machin and Derek Chatterton but I had not paid much attention to that class.

Everything seemed to be coming together rather well for me and often I'd sit down to think about the established names I had beaten. My machinery was as good as I could possibly have hoped for at my age, Don and Frank were behind me one hundred per cent and I was determined to make my mark among the world's elite the following season.

Besides, I needed some money because I had packed up all of my jobs to concentrate full time on the sport.

No screen but a keenness for winning. This time it's an international win in Spain on his 250cc Bultaco.

The Young Professional

When people start to pay you attention then things are looking up. I knew I was getting better all the time but a few folks were trying to make out I was the new boy wonder. Even if, with every race, my style and skill improved, there was still a long way to go when I made that big decision to try the world championships. My ambitions weren't too immense; a useful season in Europe was about all I could hope for although the Suzuki was still adequate enough to deal with many challengers who sometimes seemed to just make up the numbers.

The debt on the Suzuki was a long way from being cleared but I knew I needed reasonable transport for my Suzuki and Yamaha. Don was going abroad with me too. So I splashed out on a Ford Transit van although it gave me a lot of trouble. Fortunately, some necessary wins in the early part of the season made me a few bob and I was able to pay Don some wages. Knowing him I'm sure he would have gone to the Grands Prix with me for nothing even though he had given up a well-paid electrician's job.

My morale was sky-high before leaving Britain. I was doing well in both the 125cc and 250cc British Championships, although they were of little meaning to me then and I was quite pleased with the capabilities of the new 250cc twin-cylinder racer which I had specially track-tested in Spain. The Spanish concern had got over their grumpiness from the previous year and were now keen to get me to race this machine in the classics on a regular basis.

But I was never over-concerned about the Derbi and I

could choose whether I wanted to race it or not. The first time we took it out was in the Austrian GP at the Salzburg-ring. It developed a terrible misfire when I was lying second and the bike eventually gave up the ghost. Without appearing to have too large a 'north and south', I still reckon I could have had a win on my first 250cc world championship ride that day if the Derbi had been reliable. The race winner, Silvio Grassetti wasn't too far ahead of me on his MZ when I was on the gas on my water-cooled two-stroke. I definitely fancied another go on it.

But although I was called a works Derbi rider, it was the 125cc class that I was really there for. The Austrian organisers had reckoned my three rides were worth about £100 and so Don and I checked into a swishy hotel in the mountains near the track the night before the meeting. It meant that we would be in reasonable physical shape for the big day. Mind you, we still ate like hippies, a can of beans one day, maybe a frugal salad the next. And after the blow-out in the hotel, it was back to the back of the van and two cold sleeping bags. All the money had gone. There was about enough cash to buy fuel to get us to the next German round.

We didn't have to do much work on the 34-brake horse-power Suzuki to have her ready and when I finished second fastest in practice to the hot tip Nieto, prospects looked promising. So after we bombed away, I tried to act cool, maybe too cool. Nieto on the works Derbi, Gilberto Parlotti on a Morbidelli and Dieter Braun, who was on a Suzuki, were showing the way — but I was with them and as the 70-mile race wore on, I fancied I could surprise all of these big names. My machine was matching theirs in every way. All there was to be done was for me to outride them.

But I made a cock-up of the race. The last corner before the finish proved my mount could really make up lot of ground on the others and so my plan was to leave the winning burst until the last lap. It would look spectacular.

But on the hill before the final bend, a stretch where I needed to get slip-stream from the others because of the high-gearing on my bike, I went the wrong side in passing a tail-ender and let Nieto and Parlotti get away by 20 yards.

There was then no-one to slip-stream and I had no time to make up the leeway completely. But I came in third and there was practically no distance between the three of us at the flag.

We had been swopping places all the time and I was so confident that I could do it after a while, I was sitting up on the bike.

The other two should have been inches behind me if I had worked my tactics correctly. But it was a genuine mistake on my part and it made me realise that, in the level of racing I now found myself in, there was absolutely no room for rider error. Ten points, however, for third place were not to be scoffed at and the feeling that I could do well in the following Grands Prix was also shared by the British pressmen there.

The 350cc class was incredible. In practice on my Yamaha, I gave Giacomo Agostini, the reigning world champion, something to think about by qualifying only half a second slower then he did on the MV. It was un heard of then for anyone to get within three seconds of him. Jarno Saarinen, rated as one of the best riders around then, was third fastest but I was around three seconds quicker than he was. When it came to the actual race, I shot away at the start — and soon came to a halt when the gear linkage broke just as I made the first change.

The first Grand Prix may not have shown me to be a sensation but I regarded my start as a useful one and I was getting over the shock of finding myself in the big-time at the age of twenty. But Grand Prix life was so pleasant and good, that's how it felt for me. Other riders were having problems over what they considered wasn't enough start money or the conditions of the paddocks were not up to scratch and all things like that but I was just glad to be racing among top-class riders, although I did become a member of the Grand Prix Riders Association to help all competitors get as fair a deal as was possible.

The opposition in the 125cc class at first appeared really heavy but when I took pole position in practice in the next world championship round in West Germany, I thought my big moment was about to happen. This time there would be no error on my part.

Everything went well from the start. I knew Nieto was behind me in second place and all I had to do was keep that Suzuki sweetly singing round the Hockenheim track. Nieto went from view and before I could even think about how nice it would be to win, a sprocket went in my gearbox and I became just another spectator. That Suzuki was nearly always super-reliable. It just had to let me down when victory was in sight.

That Grand Prix was bad news for me all the way along the line. In the practice for 250s I experienced the worst moment I had had up to then in my racing career. When coming off the start-finish straight into the 100 mph-plus right-hander in fifth gear, the Derbi seized on both cylinders. Situations like that are not too good on the nerves! The clutch lever was just whipped in, in the nick of time, before the bike tried to get out of control.

When the Derbi did exactly the same thing to me on the same stretch of the track in the actual race just as I was catching the leaders Phil Read and Rod Gould, I nearly bust myself. Once is enough in a meeting but happening twice — and getting away with it — is quite incredible.

The prospect of a bike seizing up didn't worry me although, in common with most sensible two-stroke riders, I kept a finger on the clutch lever in case of emergencies. But lock-ups were never a great problem especially when I rode my Yamahas. Yet, when braking heavily at the approach to corners, a lot of riders had their Yams nip up after crashing down through the gearbox. They were looking for engine braking which was not there on a two-stroke and without giving the throttle a blip, there was no petroil mixture going in to lubricate the motor at a time when it was really working double overtime. That's when seizures could happen.

I knew I shouldn't be disappointed after the West German round because I did not set out with the thought of being a world-beater. But I was annoyed that on two occasions I could have collected fifteen points to go well clear in the 125cc class. Even with the 250, I must have been up with the front-runners if my luck had been in.

Not to worry. There were plenty more classics to come but the next one happened to be somewhere I didn't want to go — the Isle of Man. As a young lad, there was enjoyment in seeing the aces zoom round. But when it came to actually racing there I wasn't in the slightest bit interested.

I didn't want to race there in '71. It was only because of the points situation that I went in place of Dieter Braun. I hated every single miserable minute of that TT, from the time I got off the ferry boat until the moment I stepped back on it again. My mind was made up after that. For me it would definitely be the first and last TT and there was absolutely no way anything or anybody would get me back there to race motorcycles.

It was interesting for me to watch a TT, but I was not involved with it as a youngster. When I went as a competitor I realised what a big rip-off the whole thing was.

One point should be made loud and clear to everyone who has called me all kinds of names for not racing there after that one bad trip. The Mountain circuit did not frighten me in any way. No circuit frightens me.

I just couldn't see the sense of riding around in the pissing rain completely on your own against a clock. It wasn't racing to my mind. It was more like a special test in the International Six Days Trial — and almost as bumpy in some places.

Money had no influence or bearing on my decision not to return there. There have been some tempting offers made to me to race there after '71. Take 1973. I'm pretty sure I could easily have got £4,000 to ride there. But, after '71 I just didn't want to know and now the ACU never bother to contact me because they know they're wasting their time talking to me about the TT.

The TT is no proof of anything, in my opinion. All it is is to show how well you know the circuit. You have to be a competent rider, for sure, but take Charlie Mortimer for instance. He wins in the Isle of Man most times but mostly anywhere else — up to the 1976 classics — he didn't do much at all.

It seemed to be so cold and wet and miserable when I was there and even when I was third fastest in the 125cc practice, after doing only six laps, my heart just wasn't in the event.

Flat out on the 500cc Suzuki in 1971.

Because I took over Dieter Braun's entry at the last minute, I was forced to race his machine instead of mine but that's not to say I could have done better on my own Suzuki.

I know I was leading at one stage on the first lap of the 125cc race but then I hit fog. Fancy meeting that kind of weather in a world championship round. Over-use of the clutch because the bike had such a narrow power band cracked one of the clutch plates and when the thing bit too fiercely just after Quarter Bridge, the back wheel jumped out and I was sitting helpless on the road.

Britain's young lion was what one paper had called me. If anyone had seen my face as I got up from that prang, my expression must have seemed very animal-like. What a dump, I was thinking at that moment.

On top of it all, I was then having to fork out a lot of money just to be there and also paying an entry fee to have a chance of being peeled off a brick wall. Why on earth was it a world championship round? There were dozens of no-name wonders in the entry list when I was there and it was meant to be the British Grand Prix, our important stage of the classics.

My start money fee was worth no more than brass washers, and for the average bloke, his bike would just about be nackered after a TT. Compare that with a major European round where the start fee could be well into three figures and the circuit would be just about learned in a dozen laps.

My opinion of the TT wasn't boosted by my experience in the Production race in '71 either. On an Eddie Crooks 250cc Suzuki, I remember I did not do too badly in practice and was feeling my way in the race itself. The bike then went into an awful wobble. Oh mother, I recall saying to myself at the time. Clinging tight to the machine, the fuel tank worked loose and then, when trying to fix that, the seat seemed to move about. The bike was swaying, I was swearing and all different parts appeared to be working loose one after another. One lap was enough. Even a co-operative marshal who wanted me to lash the loose parts together couldn't persuade me to go out again. That was my lot. I didn't want any more of that business thank you very much.

My sanity was restored when I wheeled my bike out at Mallory for the Post-TT meeting. A proper race run in safe conditions with the right rewards. I know a lot of people, especially those die-hard TT-goers, have called me everything because I gave up going to the Isle of Man. Well it doesn't make me any less of a racer for not going. Those people will worry far more about it than I will, that's definitely true.

I know at that Mallory event, the old excitement came rushing back. The two wins that I had and a useful romp with Agostini on a 500cc Suzuki Seeley put me back in the right frame of mind for the next real round of the world championships — in which I was getting a little anxious for points.

The floor of an oily Transit Van isn't the best place to get a good kip and I do like a nice sleep in something resembling a bed. So I thought it was worth taking out a spot of hire purchase to buy a caravan which I could tow behind the van to all the distant meetings. Now that was better. Don and I could sleep and eat in comfort and most of the time Paul Smart and his mechanic shared it with us. There were some really funny moments when we all got together; talk about the life and soul of the paddocks!

Next, it was time to renew my rivalry with little Nieto again, this time at Assen in the Dutch TT. The size of the crowds there staggered me as they did in the previous German round. There was nothing remotely like this back at home and it took me a while to get used to all those people. In practice there were 40,000 who paid to get in; on race day the numbers swelled to around 150,000. Try getting that many around a British circuit.

Angel and myself were almost as close together in our 125cc race. After Parlotti had his Morbidelli seize and we dropped Bo Jansson back, Angel and I had a great scrap with him winning by two seconds. My Suzuki was still quick, although, now and again, it was beginning to show its age while Angel's new engine in his Derbi proved to be just that bit better.

With a run of mechanical problems, I was starting to fade way out of the picture in the 250cc class but, in the Dutch, I showed I could not be forgotten. I was about to push up to sixth place past Marsovszky on his Yamaha when the right-hand suspension unit broke away from its mounting. It looked a highly dangerous moment but I was just able to control the unpredictable Derbi twin and came to a standstill. The race was only two laps old.

We tootled across the border to Belgium and after seeing the ultra-fast Francorchamps public roads circuit, I was keen on my chances of consolidating my second place in the world championship table. Dad had come across from London specially to see me so I wanted to impress him. My girl friend Lesley was there too.

The night after first practice I decided to have a cruise around Spa just up the road for a few drinks and a laugh. But on the way back, just as I was heading down the course to the paddock, the Transit ran out of diesel. Anyway I managed to retrieve the situation by topping up the system but a fair amount of fuel slopped onto the track. It was my luck to have a Belgian copper witness this and he fined me about £6.60 on the spot for spoiling the road. A few of the riders gave me some black looks the following day too, when they had to negotiate the slippery patch first time out.

The day before the big race, my Suzuki was acting kind of strange. The power would not quite be there all the time but once dad got his hands on it, the little twin was back on song. I was away to a good start which obviously is one of the most important things to achieve and once it was signalled that Angel had retired on the third lap, I was out on my own.

Having led from the start and with no-one about me for most of the 61 miles, the race tended to drag on. The Suzuki began to misfire on the final lap and I was praying for the bike to keep going. But it did — and I had won my first Grand Prix.

Once I had crossed the finishing line, I could hardly contain myself. I wanted to get drunk, kiss as many girls as I could lay my hands on and just dance with joy. That was the proudest moment of my life up to then and, even if I had been told I had just won a million pounds on the pools, winning that first Grand Prix would still have given me more satisfaction.

My speeds surprised me. I certainly didn't think I had been going fast enough to smash the 125cc lap record and the race record. In averaging just over 110 mph I had bust Dave Simmonds' old race record by three seconds and had somehow managed to lop seven seconds off the 1969 lap record.

Winning that race gave me the most pleasure; not the fact that I was then leading the world championship. It was great to be up there but I needed no-one to tell me that only breakdowns were keeping Angel from being the undisputed leader.

His Derbi was better than my machine all through the campaign and, although there was possibly little between us when it came to riding ability, he had the advantage over me. My reign at the top would only be brief, of that I was convinced, so I wanted to make the most of the situation.

My start money fees slightly improved after that win. Not by much because I was still relatively unheard of. And as I was still a new boy, I had much more to do to prove myself as a quality international rider. Besides, the 125cc class didn't attract much money from organisers. It was and always will be the big bikes that called the tune over appearance money. In those days, the MV was much more of a draw than, say, the Morbidelli.

My start money payments must have averaged about £50 a time in '71 and so I made nothing out of the game for that year after lessening the debt on my bike, van and caravan.

I was quoted in one of the motorcycling papers at the time as saying there was more to life than just money. That was perfectly true then. Racing was fun. It still is and always will be as far as I'm concerned. My attitude may have become more professional over the years since that season but my aim will remain the same: Enjoy it.

Following the 125cc victory celebrations, I had to cool down for the 250cc race in which I took out my Yamaha for its 1971 classic baptism after the Derbi had developed vibration troubles. It made no difference to my 250 luck. Within a lap I was touring in with the Yam's oil seals gone.

Back in the paddock I was about to toast my 125cc success again when I heard that Morbidelli had slapped in a protest. They were claiming my bike had more than the regulation six gears, exactly the same thing Derbi complained about the previous year. Naturally, their protest was rejected and so it was two fingers to them.

East Germany was my next stop, the first time I had been into a Communist state and I can't say I was particularly impressed with their set-up in life. There was some squabbling over start money at this round too and I know they did increase their offer substantially after nearly every rider stated quite bluntly they would not ride. I was one of them on that occasion. But my purpose in driving hundreds of miles and even enduring primitive paddock living conditions was not the lure of cash. It was to try to earn world championship glory. The rewards might

Leader of the pack. Sheene (Yamaha) leads Jarno Saarinen (24), Guyla Marsovsky (32), Rod Gould and John Cooper at Silverstone in '71. He won.

possibly come later when I had achieved my short-term ambitions. Yet the puny amounts the East Germans were offering were just laughable and, although bargaining at the last opportunity does little good for the image of road racing, we had to make a stand.

A quarter of a million people were reckoned to be at the Sachsensring that hot, humid day. Angel was out determined to recover his pride and I knew I would have to work overtime to beat him.

In training, Nieto was a couple of seconds quicker than me but the Swede Jansson was almost five seconds faster on his Maico. I only had thoughts of the Spaniard. It was him or me for the world title and that was the way I looked at it all through the Grand Prix season.

Braun and Jansson were in the fray for a while until Angel and I resumed our personal battle over twelve laps. This time we seemed to be racing closer together than ever before. It was fantastic. There were moments when spectators lost sight of me because I was completely in the same level position as him. We swopped first and second places all the way to the end and once our fairings scraped at 100 mph on a right-hand bend. Then, with the flag in sight after the last bend, he drifted across me, I had to ease off the power and his well-used tactics had won him the race. But that was a cracker and the final result, I felt, was irrelevant even though it was 0.4 of a second that separated us.

I had always tried to keep well clear of the next man in case he took you with him if he slipped up. Certainly the dangerous points on any circuits are at slow corners when you're trying to overtake on the outside. The other rider may apply too much power coming out of the bend and his back wheel can kick round at you.

But on this occasion with Nieto, I knew I couldn't let him get away with an inch because of his superior motor. If he had fallen off, quite likely he would have sent me tumbling too. We were that near each other. The important thing for any racer to do is roll off the throttle and not lock on the brakes in cases of emergency when a rider comes off ahead of you. That's the way I act if there's enough space.

If Angel's baulking tactics were meant to dishearten me, it didn't work. I was happy enough with second place and I was still leading the honours race. Even in the 250cc event I put up a spirited performance by coming sixth on my Yamaha which was way down on power output.

The Derbi was still back at the factory in Spain where engineers had diagnosed the vibrations troubles as being caused by metal fatigue in the frame. Anyhow, they were completely rebuilding the whole lot and so I was fairly interested to see how it would fare next time out even though I was almost completely out of the title chase.

Back at the Belgian GP, I was approached by Kreidler to race off their 50cc bikes in the Czechoslovakian round at Brno to help out their works rider Jan de Vries, because he was finding the going tough against Nieto and Parlotti on the works Derbis.

Czecho was the next round so I thought it would be a nice way to earn some cash and I wouldn't have to do any work on the machine. But it was problems nearly all the way at first. I was in some pain from my sore gums and I arranged to have some antibiotics brought over from England with Ted Macauley, a reporter on the *Daily Mirror,* which helped slightly.

But when I came to practise on the mini-Kreidler, I found it a very strange proposition. The placing of the gear-lever and brake pedals confused me, there seemed not enough room to tuck my knees in and I was bloody sure the tiny tyres wouldn't hold the bike to the road in the pouring rain.

In the beginning I thought I had no chance of being able to ride it competitively but I kept plugging away and from being one of the slowest I turned in the second fastest practice time behind my old friend Nieto. And that was my first outing on a 50.

On race day, I overslept and was peacefully dreaming away about blondes when the Kreidler team came looking for me. The banging on the caravan shook me out of my sleep and I jumped into my cold leathers and shot out to the bike waiting for me on the starting grid.

When we set off, I think I gave a huge yawn; I was still half asleep. But I buzzed round as quick as I could in the wet with my head thumping and my teeth chattering with cold. When the 'GO' sign came up, I hurried on past Nieto for a win I would have suggested would have been impossible after my first practice ride on it. The winning margin was over a minute and a half. It was ridiculous the way things went for me with that bike.

By that time, I was a dedicated heavy smoker and, as I often got the craving for a fag on the start line, I drilled a hole in the bottom piece of my full-face helmet so that I could poke one through to my mouth. When it was time to start I'd cover the hole with sticky tape to stop the wind coming in. That was a good invention but I reckon some officials frowned on me smoking just as the race was to begin.

All my luck in Brno that year must have gone in the 50cc race because I had an awful start in the important 125cc event and could only get up to third. In the 250cc race, I was as high as second when the Yamaha gearbox packed up.

Nieto was now back in the championship lead in the 125cc class and if I had designs on becoming the youngest-ever world-title winner I would have to comfortably win the next two rounds in Sweden and Finland. Dad flew over specially to help me rebuild the Suzuki motor before the Swedish.

Although Don would take charge of the frame parts and look after the gearing, I would be responsible for preparing the motors. Then there could be only one person to blame if the engine developed trouble that was the fault of a mechanic's error.

In Sweden, my start was good and clean but all the time I was waiting for the Derbi of Nieto to come by me. Sure enough he did and I had one mighty job on my hands trying to stay with him. My stroke of fortune came on the fourteenth lap when plug gremlins eliminated Angel and I went on to an easy win.

Kreidler, liking what they saw in Czecho, gave me another ride in Sweden on their 50cc machine but, with bearing trouble, I reckon I did well to get into fourth place. The 250cc race was a rub-out for me when a big gaping hole appeared in the Yamaha's expansion chamber. That Yam's unreliability record never seemed to get better. Next meeting in Finland a gearbox oil seal failed.

The Finnish GP was virtually a walk-over for me. Nieto went out soon after the start and I was left to saunter home at an average speed of 81.5 mph. Now everyone was hailing me as the likely world champion. They were saying that Nieto had to do so much and pick up so many points in the final two rounds and they completely overlooked the fact that I had to do a fair bit still to preserve my 19-point lead.

As I have said, there wasn't really a time in '71 when I thought I was to become a world champion but it would have been nice if I had been fully fit for the run-in. Maybe it would have made little difference because Nieto's bike was too hot on pace for me.

If the Belgian GP win was the highspot of my early career, the darkest hours were caused by a bad crash in Holland. In fact that was about the first time I had broken a major bone while racing. Looking back, it's always easy to be wise after the event, but I know I made a mistake to borrow a 125cc Suzuki for an international meeting at Hengelo. The thing chucked me off at speed and the broken arm and chipped ankle bone were just what I didn't want at such an important time of the season.

But it made no difference whatsoever to the result in the Italian GP at Monza where Parlotti won with Nieto second and poor old me third on the short-of-wind Suzuki.

No, the injuries did not affect that one, even though I was wearing a metal wrist cuff and an ankle plaster but they did hamper my bid to squeeze the title out of Angel's grasp in the final round in Spain.

The sequence of events which showed the young hopeful giving the wily grand prix campaigner a long, hard fight and subsequently climaxing in something of a breathtaking finish would have made an ideal film script if we had been more glamorous than small bike, small money racers.

My kiss goodbye to the world championship award went largely with a heavy crash at Mallory in the September Race of the Year meeting. A tyre went at Gerrards Bend and I was flung into a bank. The hospital I was taken to in the ambulance from the track examined me and discharged me on the grounds that I had suffered no damage. I even had an X-ray. But the pain was terrible for days afterwards and I could barely move. The doctor was called to our home in Holborn and he immediately said I should be in hospital.

There was no chance of that. I had to get out to Spain to sort out Nieto who needed to win to clinch the title.

My bike and other raceware had gone out with Phil Read and I just took a basic survival kit with me when I flew out from Heathrow airport — toilet requisites and a clean pair of socks and pants plus plenty of cigarettes.

To add to my troubles I had contracted to race the Kreidler again. They were paying for various expenses such as my hire car and air ticket and I needed something to defray the flight costs. Feeling terrible and looking even worse, I somehow achieved second place during the race. Then a crankshaft went on the last lap.

That didn't bother me. I was glad that I didn't crash and put myself in any further pain. On the way back to the pits from where I left the Kreidler I stopped for a drink of water in one of those fountains that Spain seems to have hundreds of. As I craned my body over the side, a rib twanged out, one that I had broken at Mallory. A strange sight that, so I thought it best go back and I forced the protruding bone into place in the rib cage. Back in the paddock, strips of tape around my torso held the thing in and I was all wrapped like a parcel, before the 125cc race, the decider.

But at one stage the previous day, it looked as if I might have to scratch from the race when a disc valve broke in practice. Dad was with me but we had brought over no spares. But Jan De Vries who had taken the 50cc championship, with a bit of help from me I liked to think, very kindly offered to make one for us. We had the machine together again ready just in time but, without any opportunity to test the Suzuki, we just had to trust it would be OK.

The Suzuki went well enough and it was again the usual four faces sorting it out at the front — Nieto, Jansson, Braun and myself. Dieter went out first with a blown head gasket on his Maico, then it was Jansson falling by the wayside with collapsed rear wheel bearings.

So it was me and my old mate Angel once more. He had done something nasty to his foot in an earlier race so he could not have been feeling too bright. I certainly wasn't OK as we hared about under the sun at Jarama.

Just as we were getting near the final dash home, I spun round on some oil at one of the bends. I slid gracefully on my backside and before I could get back into the groove, Nieto had whistled away and Chas Mortimer had sneaked into second.

The end of that year was disappointing. Nieto was champion and I was second and I should have been nothing but delighted with my first try at the big-time. But I couldn't help wondering what might have happened if I had not fallen off in Spain . . . or if I had pipped Nieto in East Germany . . . or if my bike had been as quick as his. But there was no point in dallying over the final outcome; it was all over for another year but I was not too sure whether another season in the same class would do my racing career any benefit.

Upon returning home I found out the true extent of my injuries received at Mallory: a compression fracture of three vertebrae and five broken ribs. No wonder I was in anguish whenever I walked.

The races I had in Britain in between the Grands Prix were largely successful and I reckon the best performance was at Silverstone where I had a terrific dice with Jarno Saarinen, Marsovszky, Rod Gould and John Cooper in the 250cc race on my Yamaha. I won, but a handkerchief could almost have covered us at the end.

Things were looking up all the time for me in the closing months of '71 and I jumped at the chance to go to ride in the United States. Gene Romero had promised to fix me up with rides in the Ontario meeting when he stayed in London but the Seeley Yamahas I rode all packed up in the three races I competed in.

It's true to say that hardly at any time, was I riding flat out; most of the time it was eight-tenths capacity. There was always plenty in hand.

But it was a fantastic year for me. It set me up for what looked a promising career and I was getting bags of publicity in the motorcycling press. The sport was still a bit non-U in those days in the eyes of the national daily papers, so even though I nearly pinched a world crown, few people outside the game knew about this Briton's exploits.

The first Grand Prix victory. A salute from Barry on his 125cc Suzuki as he crosses the line first in the 1971 Belgian GP at Francorchamps. He also set the record lap for his class.

Agony All the Way

We had always been a close-knit family. Coming from the heart of London meant that, by tradition, we would always boast a good relationship between ourselves. So it came as something of a shock to learn one afternoon that sister Margaret had secretly married racer Paul Smart at Maidstone registry office in Kent.

I mean it wasn't entirely unexpected that the two would get hitched some day; it just took us all by surprise that they should do it without warning. Mum would have liked to have seen her married off in the grand manner, all flowing lace and church service and all that. But she wasn't upset. Mum knew that if Maggie was happy, then she would be too.

As for me I was getting myself mentally tuned up for the big year of 1972 that lay ahead. I had a Yamaha contract in my pocket, not a full, big money one but a worthwhile one all the same. It was certainly the first occasion a manufacturer was paying me to ride on a regular basis in the world championships.

After my successful year in 1972, lots of offers were flying around, Suzuki wanted me to race their 500cc air-cooled twin at certain British meetings as I did the previous year and they were talking about getting a 750cc water-cooled three-cylinder job for me to ride. Derbi must have been pleased about my performances in '71 and they were interested in getting me to ride their improved 250cc twin. Ducati were another factory after me. It was all building up very nicely and I was cock-a-hoop.

Everything was going right and I had no reason to believe my good fortune could change. I gratefully seized the opportunity to contest the South African meetings that winter along with the rest of the travelling British brigade of Ray Pickrell and Paul Smart. It was glorious out there in the hot sun. Days would be spent lazing round swimming pools, between meetings, and I reckoned that the good life suited me right down to the ground.

Looking back over that year, it would seem to me that the trip to South Africa sowed the seeds of my over-confidence. I thought after going out there and with a great season behind me in the world championships I could become one of the greats of racing. But, at the same time, I was expecting it all to come rather easily. Complacency had set in and I was going to pay the full price for it in the months ahead.

I had my first real go on the 250cc Yamaha twin in South Africa. Although it was still much of an experimental machine, this works water-cooled Yamaha was intended to be the bike to do well in the world championships. In the 250cc race at the South Africa TT at Pietermaritzburg, I came in third behind a couple of the local lads but in the next ride at Kyalami I had to quit the race because of handling problems. So it was early days with the bike but, at Kyalami, I was timed as clocking over 129 mph on the Yam — faster than anyone else.

In fact it was the 500cc Suzuki that I did best on in South Africa. I was second to Ago in the TT, although it was by a long chalk, and I had a fifth at the other meeting.

But I chose to stick with Yamaha. It gave me the opportunity to move into a bigger capacity racing in two classes and with the name of Yamaha behind me I thought I was just about made. My water-cooled 250cc and air-cooled 350cc were almost identical to those that would be raced by Rod Gould. Phil Read and Jarno Saarinen would also be Yamaha-mounted. Quite an exciting battle in store, I imagined.

My first official outing on the 250 was at Mallory Park.

Even though it was damp and quite slippery, conditions I am not keen on at all, I won the 250cc race easily and I think I would have taken the 500cc race too had not Barry Randle and I touched while approaching the hairpin. I didn't damage myself too badly at all but crashing in the first meeting of the season is never a good omen.

But people were talking about me, which was good. My hair was long and my habits were apparently trendy and so that helped to give me a bit of a following with the public. That year I started to wear a posh set of white leathers. That was because of my contract with Rivetts who supplied them. A fan club also started up that year.

But, being an ambitious lad, there was only thing I wanted to win — a world championship title. I had almost done it the year before. Why shouldn't I do it this year on quality raceware? Thinking I was as good as men like Saarinen and Read was not out of character for me. Before Saarinef became a sensation, I beat him nearly every time in '71, but to actually think I could achieve the brilliance and international respect commanded by those riders at the time without a great deal of effort was not the thoughts of the real me. I was to be punished for my rather casual approach that season.

I knew it would be tough. Grands Prix generally are. And I would get no help from my Yamaha team-mates. There were no team instructions. It was every man for himself. If it had been any other way, I wouldn't have looked at the Yamaha contract. I ride to win and would never ever take orders to finish second to a team-mate. I'm number two to nobody.

I always think of the time little Bill Ivy cut his motor at Creg-ny-Baa while leading the 125cc Isle of Man TT purposely to let Phil Read win on factory orders. I would never be involved in that kind of situation. That's not even racing. Poor old Bill. Like a lot of other admirers, I felt sorry for him that day especially as Read didn't appear to set out to be a friendly team-mate.

My act at the beginning of '72 was completely together. I had even devised a new Sheene gimmick that I thought would go down well with the crowds — the V for victory sign, a Churchillian-type gesture that I was often to use when leading certain big races. The idea stemmed from an American transfer on my bike fairing which showed a hand painted in the stars and stripes of the United States giving an upward V sign.

By the time the Easter Brands meeting came along, I knew I was right on the ball. I became King of Brands in winning the 250cc and 500cc races and that win on the 356cc Yamaha was my first ever victory in a 500cc class event. Just as I clobbered the opposition in Britain in '71 on my 125cc Suzuki, I was doing the same with the 250 boys on my Yamaha. It was going well, I was going well. Now for those world titles, I thought.

When I was brought off through a seizure while track testing the bikes at Le Mans in France prior to the opening classic I accepted it as being just a hazard of finding out ways and means of improving the machinery . . . I hurt my back there.

At the first Grand Prix of the season at the Nurburgring in West Germany, I was a little disappointed to say the least about my initial showing. I collected no points in either the 250cc or 350cc races. I made four laps in the 250 and then went out with a broken ignition earth wire and a back wheel on the point of breaking up, and could only circuit twice in the other race before a seizure stopped any more travel. Even in practice, I couldn't get in the top six fastest riders.

I remember in practice we had all sorts of weather conditions, snow, sunshine, mist, the lot, and as one of the training sessions was right early in the morning when I'd still usually be tucked up in bed, I began to wheel out Saarinen's Yamaha thinking, in my dozy state, that the machine was mine.

That was only the opening round, so I still fancied my chances of being among the points at the next round in France. But at the Clermont Ferrand circuit, I began to sense that the magical route to the top would not be so easy.

My caravan had to be parked some way from the track's catering facilities and coupled with my thoughts being focused on the need for points, I was going without food for long spells. This, I'm sure, led to the dizziness I was experiencing and I didn't know whether I was coming or going at certain times. I had switched to the other air-cooled 250cc Yamaha because the so-called new water-cooled machine was not producing the goods. And to cap it all, the French organisers missed my flying lap in practice and only after laying out 50 Francs as the official protest fee did I get my rightful start on the grid. The dizzy spells seemed to get worse, though, and deciding discretion was the better part of valour, even in such a vital meeting, I gave the two races a miss.

The world championship dream was turning into night-mare and not even the fourth place in the Austrian Grand Prix on my obviously slower Yamaha in the 250cc race did much for my sinking hopes. At that meeting at Salzburg-ring, I had had a flat tyre, an assortment of mechanical problems and a lashing around my leg from the chain after the spring link broke. Ironical thing about this race was that it was won by Bo Jansson on the same works Derbi I had originally turned down.

What was happening to me? These Yamahas, I had originally thought, were superior machines and yet I was doing nothing. Riding like an old woman didn't help matters either.

Friction between me and Yamaha mechanics was gradually building up. I'd suggest one or two ways in which the bikes could be improved and they would look at me with a pained expression as if to say, 'Who's this cocky bugger telling us what to do?'

The Italian Grand Prix at Imola in '72 was the bad one. A really black smudge on my copybook. It was a seizure in practice on the 250cc. Up the road I went and eventually ended up in St. Bartholomew's Hospital in London with a badly broken left collar-bone that needed close medical attention. The crash also put a deep cut into my stomach and left me dazed for what seemed days.

It was a bad break with the bone all split and cracked and it was to take the longest of any injury to clear up. Just after I had been released from hospital, I was driving in London and had to slam on the brakes to avoid crashing into a car that had pulled out in front of me. The sudden jerk pulled out the injured bone and I was back to square one again.

But even though I was in pain around the shoulders, I wanted to keep racing and so I chose to ride at the Post-TT meeting at Mallory. The hospital wanted me to have an operation that particular day to take out a bone splinter which was preventing the collar-bone from properly knitting together. I told them I'd be coming in during the evening because I'd be out for the day. As it happened, I did nothing at Mallory except ride in a fair amount of agony from my strapped-up shoulders.

If anything did annoy me it was the British National Health system. It took them over three weeks before deciding I needed an operation. That meant I was three weeks longer out of racing. With my luck at the time, I was perhaps just as well off in hospital!

The operation went successfully although the recuperation period should have been longer than I allowed for and

79

in my comeback Grand Prix in Sweden I just had to pull out of both 250cc and 350cc races because of my aching shoulder.

Further mechanical bothers eliminated me from the Finnish GP and, by then, I had just about decided that this arrangement with Yamaha would soon be ending. There were a few wins here and there and some good placings in international meetings at home and abroad; in one at Brands I managed to finish second ahead of Ago. It wasn't until the final GP round in Spain that I collected my highest classics 250cc placing with a third behind Renzo Pasolini and Tepi Lansivuori. In the 350cc race, I was holding third when the top hose union broke.

Even though Saarinen was really going like a dream then, I felt I could get a good placing on the 350cc Yamaha in the Race of the Year at Mallory. That's always a good race to win. But a crankshaft went before I could really get going. I did make amends slightly by winning the 500cc race, one of several late season wins I had in that class.

But the season was a disaster for me, one to be erased from the memory. The whole of 1972 put me back a couple of years and did absolutely nothing for my reputation.

Nothing before or after remotely compared with that season. It was a bad move to go Yamaha. I found the machines unreliable, in many cases, uncompetitive and the relationship with the Yamaha hierarchy deteriorated all the while. So not wanting to make people think that the cause of the Yamaha's failure was my fault, I left to join Suzuki. They could keep the Yamahas.

It was just a boring, horrible year. I wanted the 500-4 Yamaha but there was no chance and the bikes they gave me were rubbish. The two standard bikes I had in Britain were OK; I was winning almost everything until I went away to ride the water-cooled 250cc.

On the domestic front, I was then living in a self contained one-bedroomed flat on my own back in my old stamping ground of Holborn. I had spotted the old farm-house at Walton Highway, near Wisbech in Cambridge-shire, which had been lying empty for eight years and extensive repairs and renovations were taking place on it. As it was a big place, I wanted my parents to live there and that meant dad could retire a few years earlier than normal from his job.

I realised at the end of the year, I would have to put much more into my racing to get a satisfactory return and 1972 will always be the year that brought me down to earth with a big bump. When the success wasn't there it also taught me who my real friends were in racing.

The Suzuki 750-3 on which Sheene won the FIM Formula 750 Championship in 1973. But although he rounds the Mountside hairpin at Scarborough in front of Mick Grant, Sheene retired with jammed front forks and Grant won on his debut on the John Player Norton.

81

Off Into Europe

Being the best in the world at any sport is the ultimate goal of all ambitious top-level competitors. I was only twenty when I first set out on the long and winding road to the world crown. And I reckoned I was good enough to win it even though I had been racing for just a few short seasons and had a private machine that had already given its best years.

Perhaps I was cocky about my chances. There I was, a raw young Londoner rubbing shoulders with the cream of road racing talent and with hardly two halfpennies to clink together. Events dictated that I didn't finish top man in 1971, but the whole incredible experience made me a much wiser bloke. Far from knocking the over-confident streak out of me, the whole season's excitement possibly made me even more determined to show everyone I was a world-beater.

My balloon burst in 1972 with a succession of bad things happening to me and so my ego was well deflated by the time a new season's racing in 1973 dawned.

With nothing won and a whole lot of humble pie inside me from '72, my temper wasn't improved when one or two dossers began to talk about me being sacked from Yamaha. I'll explain the circumstances surrounding my move from Yamaha to Suzuki later but I'll say here and now the excitement and old enthusiasm came flooding back when I began to piece together a machine that could do me a good turn.

The new campaign was merely a few weeks away when I was given the opportunity to build my own special 500cc Suzuki, a real do-it-yourself job. Suzuki had a batch of air-cooled 500cc twin engines sent over from the factory in

Japan to their plant in Croydon and they kindly let me pick out a good one. What an invitation! I could hardly wait to take the thing apart once it had been prised from the packing case.

Handling was the big headache at the time, so I settled for a Seeley frame and the whole plot seemed to fit in quite well. But it took so much time. I would dash down to Croydon first thing every morning and work continuously through the day and often right into the small hours of the next morning. Looking back it seems like an amazing thing to do but, after what happened the year before, I was desperate to have machinery I knew would serve me well in the coming season.

Almost every day I would work on preparing the bike much to the annoyance of my girlfriend then, Lesley Shepherd. She was a neat little blonde and we were to have a good thing going for a long time. Her complaints that she never saw me during that period were justified I suppose. Once I got back home to Holborn I would flop into bed exhausted and that kind of non-activity happened nearly every evening until my own 'personal' bike was ready.

Frank's sound advice on bikes always came in handy, and when it comes to two-stroke tuning, there were few better in the land than him. Funny thing was though, everyone thought my 500cc Suzuki was something extra special, a one-off job sent over from Japan for me to blow off the rest.

Stan Woods, then my Suzuki works team mate, couldn't believe that my bike was standard production-line stuff. 'That's never a bog-standard engine,' he exclaimed after I had won my third race on the trot. My hard work was to pay off, much to the disbelief of a lot of other rivals who also refused to accept that my mount was nothing out of the ordinary, apart from having been given the Sheene magic touch.

It was a good bike but not a world-beater. It had its

83

limitations, although it was a good match for those 350cc Yamahas.

At the time, all the talk was about Suzuki's incredible 750cc racers and reports were coming through every day of the amazing speeds being obtained on them. They had shown in 1972 that Suzuki were getting together something good in 750cc racing especially as the bikes were producing 107 bhp at the back wheel.

Then, at the beginning of '73, Ron Grant, Suzuki's works rider in Australia, was told that, during track tests at Hamamatsu, his latest bike went to 183 mph. A year before, while practising for Daytona, he managed 171 mph, so there must have been some super development work carried out.

That 183mph apparently was the quickest speed ever attained by a racing bike. Needless to say, I wanted one of those three-cylinder water-cooled jobs. It was pumping out 117 bhp and the frame was said to be better and stronger.

Racing one of those superbikes was an ambition I wanted to achieve very quickly. These were real men's bikes, not one of your mickey mouse 125cc efforts. The smaller class of racing was definitely behind me then.

Well I got one all right. But it bore hardly any likeness in performance and finish to those beauties that were tearing around at great speeds. It was nothing but a heap of rubbish, an assortment of unwanted parts put together in a hurry to resemble something like a 750cc racer. It had come over from the United States importers who must have stripped off all the good bits and fixed on all their discarded parts . . . and Suzuki GB, the go-ahead home set-up who were keen to hit Britain with this much-talked about machine, were saddled with a bum steer.

There was even more work needed to be done on that one and further burning of the midnight oil and the addition of another Seeley frame put it into something like the shape that would get it through the scrutineers check

. . . and a bit more.

Brother-in-law Paul Smart was the lucky guy, though. He jumped at the chance to join Suzuki America after being dropped from Bob Hansen's Stateside Kawasaki team and he landed one of those super-quick Suzuki-3's.

My 750cc was supposed to be 'factory-supplied' too but there was a vast difference between the two. Still, I was happy. Suzuki's plans were to contest the FIM Formula 750 championship and the Motor Cycle News Superbike championship, plus the possibility of occasional 500cc world championship rounds when there was no clash of dates.

Racing in the 750cc class had already taken off; the Transatlantic match races just about started the enthusiasm and people were beginning to take notice of this new class of bike in Europe. They were big, fast and powerful and this type of machine definitely injected new life into the British racing set-up.

Just before my first run-out of the season — at Mallory Park — when I was anxious to do well in order to start my year on the right note, I did a small photographic leather gear modelling assignment for Vogue magazine. Photographer was David Bailey of international fame. At the time, Bailey was at the centre of controversy over a feature film he had shot on that eccentric Andy Warhol. Throughout the session of picture-taking, scores of reporters were hounding Bailey about the Warhol programme and it didn't do much for my poses, I can tell you.

About the same time, I tried my hand at speedway. Along with Dave Potter, we were given some tuition at Hackney's track by Don Smith who used to ride well for West Ham and made a big name for himself in trials riding. No chance of taking that game up. Boy you really seemed to fly round those bends.

Mallory Park traditionally stages the opening meeting of

85

the season and I always usually had a successful first outing there. But I remember thinking, after suffering engine troubles in three races and getting nothing for my effort, was my ill-luck of '72 going to continue once more?

Adaptability is an important ingredient for success in the racing game, so I'm always keen to have a go at anything on two wheels. When an opportunity arose to test-ride a couple of AJS production scramblers, I was at the test track like a shot. The first time on a scrambles machine was a gas for me and reaching 50mph was fast enough. I enjoyed the experience despite all the aches and pains afterwards.

Oulton Park is one of my favourite British circuits and I can motor round there when I have to. But you wouldn't believe the confidence boost I had there after winning the two big races on the Suzukis and smashing Derek Minter's old lap record at the start of the '73 campaign. The works bikes were feeling right; I was beginning to feel right; and I sensed there might be something good at last happening for me.

My first trip abroad that year took me to Rouen in the north of France. The opposition was pretty formidable but with the F750 European championship series looming up, it would provide a useful test for me. It was also my first go on the Seeley-framed 750cc Suzuki so I was interested to see how it would shape up. Three laps after the start of the first leg I was in the pits with ignition trouble. In the second leg I fared little better, a broken gear selector shaft putting me out.

The big-money event at Imola was one I had my eye on even with all the heavies there like Saarinen and Baumann. Sixth place was the highest position I reached before retiring in both legs with clutch and chain bothers. Saarifen was the rage at that time. Everything he did was right. Such a super-cool rider and a great character around the paddocks.

There was no question in my mind that he would have taken the 500cc world championship from Ago that year. He was on the fantastic Yamaha 500-4 I wanted to ride and, in his hands, there was no-one to touch him. His death in the Italian Grand Prix was a disaster for the sport. He had proved to be the man capable of smashing the Agostini stranglehold and racing would have been all the better for that. But what a tragedy. He gave me some beatings in the past on the smaller bikes and I had enormous respect for him, as did most people connected with motorcycle racing.

My own personal performances were picking up slightly as the weeks went by; a small contribution to Britain's win over America in the Transatlantic Trophy match races; setting up a new lap record at Brands; and the odd win here and there.

But my thoughts were on the prize that was waiting to be plucked in Europe — the season-long Formula 750 Championship. It was really the biggest-capacity world championship class, although it was never given the official classic title. I can't think why it wasn't given full status because the competition was just as tough and the programme almost as demanding as the series of Grands Prix in the other classes of world championship racing.

In the first round at Imola, I collected no points. The second round at Clermont Ferrand in France I made no mistake.

It was just one twelve-lap race and after I passed Peter Williams on the monocoque Norton and John Dodds on his 350cc Yamaha on the fifth lap, it was all plain sailing for the maximum fifteen points. Mind you, the race almost didn't get off the ground. We had a hassle with the organisers about the safety aspect of the track. Those Armco barriers can look mighty frightening with only a scattering of straw bales around.

Someone got up a petition amongst the riders and the

Saucy badges decorating the leathers, Barry Sheene buys more cigarettes before racing.

threat of no racing hung over the meeting unless matters improved with more straw bales placed around the circuit.

There was a whole lot more arguing and there was even a sit-down protest by some of the lads in one race during the warm-up lap. My event fortunately did get under way although the safety standards had not improved. The organisers had their own way on this occasion but the strength and unity of rider-power had been noted.

The next day, a Bank Holiday Monday, wasn't so lucky. Along with team-mate Stan Woods, we had flown home from France in time for the King of Brands meeting. I was leading one of the big races but was being plagued with rear wheel bearing trouble. But a front wheel puncture on Hawthorn Hill ruined everything for me.

Somehow I managed to save myself from becoming a wooden overcoat job. Don't ask me how. But in smashing my right foot I tore all the toe-nails off. It sounds like some wartime torture and believe me it felt like it! As I lay back moaning and groaning waiting for the ambulance, I heard over the public address system that I retained my King of Brands crown by my placings in the other races. So the ambulance had to make a quick detour via the control tower for me to get my crown and laurels. Yet I reckon I would have swopped the prizes for my set of toe nails. My foot was giving me hell after that and so I decided to nip off to Tunisia for a holiday just lounging about, drinking and having a pleasant rest.

It was perfect cruising about among those camels but disappointments were awaiting me when I returned home to contest the post-TT races at Mallory. By rights, I should have cleaned up but a slipping clutch clobbered my hopes in two of the big races although I did manage to win one final on the 500cc.

I was losing ground in the MCN Superbike Championship, a competition which I was keen to win and I realised I would have to go some to get back in the hunt. But, above all, the Formula 750 championship was top of my list of priorities yet it was obvious men like Jack Findlay and Guido Mandracchi, both on the Suzuki Europa water-cooled three-cylinder bikes, were going to give me a rough time.

Even my team-mate Stan Woods, on a similar machine to mine, was going to be a bit of a bother but I was less worrried about his challenge. Without sounding too big-headed, I knew I could out-ride Woodie if my machine was on song. We were both riding as equals. There was no question of being Suzuki's number one rider.

Unfortunately all kinds of upsets happened to my Suzuki during the next round in Sweden and it meant that I had to settle for third place behind two of the main rivals. I pushed through into the lead after three laps of the Anderstorp circuit and was feeling really cool. Then a seal blew and engine oil got into the ignition system, the bike went onto two cylinders and I was also restricted to four gears.

Findlay flashed by me and Woodie did the same on the last but one lap. Still it was some points in the bag and I was still in the lead in the championship placings. It was still being looked upon as something of a second-rate championship. Start money and cash prizes were nothing to write home about and nearly all the Swedish round press coverage was being given over to the 500cc boys where Phil Read clinched his first title in that class.

Stopping over in Scandinavia where, as we all know, they have some terrific ladies, I had a stab at the 500cc race in the Finnish Grand Prix, my first attempt against the world championship big boys. Fifth fastest in practice about five seconds down on top man Agostini, I had hoped for a reasonably high placing and when I got up to fourth spot in my first GP of the year, I thought: 'Blimey, this is all right.' But the bloody crankshaft broke on the Suzuki and I was left to watch Ago just pip Read.

This was another meeting where riders expressed their concern about the general set-up. Our complaints were about the obstacles around the track, the road surface, the poor start money fees paid and one or two other things that combined to make the racer's lot not an altogether ideal one.

Strike action was talked about the night before but we finally decided to present a petition listing our grouses. Our actions taken that year gave warning to organisers and to the FIM that we meant business but improvements were slow in coming. Steps were taken, though, to appoint selected riders to help FIM stewards in circuit safety inspection.

Now I'm never too ruffled about whether a track's surface is rough or smooth. It's the same for everyone but, with speeds getting higher and higher, there is a limit to which bikes can be safely ridden if the road is not reasonably even. Wet weather is a different thing. It can be mighty dodgy flinging two wheels about at 150 mph and so if the surface is like a skating rink I don't get so disappointed about not finishing first. I'm reasonably courageous but not stupid! The next British meeting provided just those kind of undesirable conditions.

The Hutchinson 100 at Brands in 1973 was a stinker. It was wet and horrible and we should have all been cocooned in the clubhouse instead of trying to negotiate the circuit in the 'wrong' direction.

I like doing the anti-clockwise Brands because it makes a change from the boring short circuit which I am growing less fond of year by year. The full Brands circuit is a gem, perfect to run a Grand Prix on and so I can never understand why organisers still continue to use the 1.24 miles when they've got 2.61 miles at their disposal.

I managed to land £350 and the beautiful Mellano Trophy which is so large it just about fitted in the back of my Transit Van. But I came to grief twice during the afternoon, thankfully, with only my pride hurt. I seem to have more prangs at Brands than on any other track but twice in one meeting is some going even by my standards. The first time I slid off at Paddock Bend due to some spilt petrol, the next time at Druids after my exhaust dug into the tyre, although on the second occasion I bent the handlebars back into shape, restarted and came in eighth. Dave 'Crasher' Croxford also had a couple of falls and as I passed him while he was skidding up the road on his back he put his hand up to me and I waved back. Friendly chap, old Dave!

A few days earlier I had been on mid-week duty in Finland for the fourth round of the Formula 750 Championship at Hameenlina. I had to go out on my 500cc because the barrel was still wrecked on the 750 cc from the Swedish race and it was clear that I would have a fight on my hands with Tepi Lansivuori performing on a 350cc Yamaha in front of his own crowd.

Tepi took the lead from me after a great scrap and thinking it was better to be safe than sorry, I opted for a comfortable second place and the twelve points that went with it. Findlay took third and Woods fifth so they were still hot on my tail. But sitting on top of the table with the next round in Britain made me realise that I had a great chance to claim my first major award.

But just as in anything in life, it is dangerous to assume. Silverstone was going to produce points for me, of that I was sure. I had good experience on the airfield track and although Paul Smart was there on the red-hot Suzuki US 750 as well as Yvon DuHamel with his works 750cc Kawasaki I felt I would finish ahead of my main challengers.

The first leg proved me right. I was third behind Smartie and DuHamel and I knew a similar placing in the second leg would be ideal. But when I was ready to go at the start of the second race, my 750-3 burst a cylinder head gasket.

That meant switching to my 500 twin or becoming a spectator. The lack of power on such a fast circuit was an important factor but I wasn't too despondent over my sixth place which was only six seconds behind double winner Smart.

But Findlay was second overall compared to my fourth and so that wasn't too brilliant. But the kick in the teeth came when I was told I had broken the FIM rules by riding two different bikes in the two legs. Well that was just great! I finished up with nothing at all after flogging my guts but for over an hour at around 102 mph.

The only compensation from that meeting was the beating of Ago for the first time in the 500cc race. Boy, those fans really urged me on to pass Ago to get into second place behind Read in the closing stages. No wonder I punched my fist in the air with delight on the finishing straight.

To give credit to the Auto Cycle Union, they stuck up for me in the hassle over Formula 750cc championship points from Silverstone but the FIM, being the biggest noise, had the final say. It meant that 'Jolly Jack' Findlay was the new leader and I was in second spot.

It was perhaps a useful thing to happen to me because I was really determined to show who was best by the time the next round came round. But before then, I managed to crack the Snetterton and Scarborough 500cc lap records held by Agostoni and finally managed to win a round of the MCN Superbikes at Mallory a few days after my 23rd birthday. Just to put me in the right frame of mind I took Ago's old Cadwell lap record.

Hockenheim in West Germany staged the penultimate round in the F750 series and was to turn out to be the most vital of the whole competition. Findlay would have seemed an easy winner in the first leg to the spectators but the seventeen-second gap between him and myself was mostly due to a blown head gasket on my Suzuki. I suffered the same trouble in the second leg and crept home in fourth place. Luck was on my side in a way because poor old Findlay came off while he was again leading me.

Fourth overall was good enough to be back on my favourite perch at the top but by winning the race over the two legs, Stan Woods was putting the pressure on me in the final event seven days later. John Dodds was also very much in the hunt but it was Findlay that needed to be stopped.

So we trucked down to Barcelona and set ourselves up for my first big breakthrough. This time it was one twenty-five lap race on a twisty, up-and-down circuit in Barcelona. Franco and I worked out what I had to do — merely keep ahead of Findlay and not too far behind Dodds! When I got off the start line third from last away, the plan had gone decidedly wrong and as Dodds had shot off into the blue yonder, I looked as if I was going to lose the title at the last hurdle.

But I motored as hard as I could, wary of the slippery conditions caused by rubber on the road from the cars' practice session and ploughed my way through the field to second place after five laps. I stuck there, not risking it by having a go at catching Dodds and frequently looking out behind for Findlay, who, it turned out, was glued in fourth spot behind his team-mate Mandracchi. If Mandracchi had had more sense, he would have tried to let Findlay through to third to give him some chance of catching me. But as the gap between myself and Mandracchi was thirty seconds, I don't think he would have had a hope of getting me in sight.

So I had done it. A real champion. And I proved to everyone that I had the ability to ride a 750. There are quite a lot of knockers in racing as I suppose there are in other sports so it gave me enormous pleasure to silence those critics who were saying at the start of the season I would blow out on the big bikes.

The honour of winning the championship was about the only reward though. Financial return from being number one only amounted to a few pounds profit. But I appreciated that the big pay-outs for start money would be easier to obtain with something to shout about and I would be able to ride good quality machines in the future.

In all the excitement that was to follow in the next few years, my achievement in winning that Formula 750 title in my debut season on the superbike against quite experienced opposition tends to be overshadowed. I thought I had done rather well but most of the hullaballoo was centred on the 'proper' world championships and I don't think I truly got the recognition I deserved, although that's not meant to sound like sour grapes.

Rumours began to float around that I might go back to Yamaha and do the classics the following year. But there was nothing in that. Suzuki and I had a good relationship and I was even more pleased to hear that I might be teaming up with Paul Smart in the Grands Prix in '74 on a rather special but, as yet, secret 500cc machine.

But I had one more job to complete in '73 before I could settle down for a nice rest. That was winning the MCN Superbike Championship in the final double-points round at Brands Hatch.

A few days before the final meeting of the season, I was doing some tyre testing at Silverstone. I was really on the gas coming out of Abbey Curve, my 750cc must have been clocking 125 mph when the back wheel stepped out and I went flying. The bike caught alight and was a sorry sight. I burned my hands and copped a few bruises but nothing more serious. The cause of the crash was a big garden worm which had been crossing the track when I came hurtling through. The poor creature was squashed on the road with my tyre tread mark right over it.

That was the closest call I had all season, certainly it could have had very serious consequences. My mechanic

Don and I had to do some really hasty rebuilding on the bike to get it ready for Brands where I won the race and, thanks to Barry Scully who edged Peter Williams on the John Player Norton into fourth spot, I claimed the British Superbike crown.

Willy and myself had tied on points for the title but I had more wins than him — two to his one to be precise. That was another good competition to win, although it did appear that I sneaked through at the bell to nick it in my first year of 750 racing.

I didn't want that season to end. Everything was going for me toward the finish, just like a schoolboy's dream and when I was voted 'Man of the Year' by the world's biggest-selling bike weekly newspaper, Motor Cycle News, I kept having to pinch myself to see if it all was really happening.

A good indication of my popularity was seeing the number of people who would be around me at various events. Now I was the centre of attraction and I was lapping it up. But I'm sure quite a number of those people happy to share in the enjoyment of my success were those who reckoned I was more or less on the scrap-heap after my falls and performances the previous year.

Most of the good rides of that year stand out well in my memory and I make no apologies for blowing my own trumpet by listing the triumphs. With twenty-six major wins behind me, and being the Formula 750cc champion Superbike winner, King of Brands and 500cc Shellsport title-holder, I was proud, as were my parents and my girlfriend.

Doing that well in a season meant a lot of bread was going into my bank account. The Superbike success was worth £2,000 alone. It was definitely the year that made me realise I could make some really good money from the sport if I kept my head.

Near to the end of the season, I almost became involved in a rather serious incident, outside the Grovewood suite at

Brands where they hold official functions during and after races. This was during the presentation on the MCN Superbike Championship awards and I had just been presented with that rather grotesque figure of a man which is the prize — as well as some nice money — that goes to the winner of the series.

After the awards were handed over and the champagne was being passed around, I spotted a bloke who I had sold a bike to and was still waiting for the money. He had wanted to race pretty badly and so I thought I would do him a favour by not pressing for the money immediately. However that was some time ago and the money was not forthcoming. I cornered him and asked: 'When will I be getting the money?'

He stunned me by saying: 'I can't pay you. There's no chance of you getting the money.'

I told him I'd prefer to talk about the matter outside. When we got out there, he started being cheeky and gave me a lot of lip. The anger mounted inside me, so I grabbed him and had him across the iron railings. I wanted to break his bloody neck. If you promise somebody some money, you should always keep your word. That's my opinion and I believe it's the right one. But somebody saw what was going on and pulled me off him. Just as well. The headline wouldn't have looked good in the papers: 'New champion in punch-up.' But I'm dead against violence. Someone really needs to provoke me before I feel the need to get involved in an incident.

Machine To Beat
the World

Once I had tasted life on larger capacity machines, there was little else I wanted to race other than 500's and 750's. They oozed real power and excitement and all other size bikes seemed puny by comparison.

So I didn't need to be asked twice when the offer came up to race Suzuki's new 500cc square four, a machine the Press claimed could challenge the might of MV and Yamaha in the world championships. After giving the classics a miss the previous year I was dead keen to try to land a proper world title. There was no hesitation in signing the three contracts with Suzuki Japan, Suzuki America for the Stateside races and Suzuki GB for the home events.

The 500-4 was shown to me and my new Suzuki team-mates Paul Smart and Cliff Carr, the Briton who raced in the States for long periods, in early '74 at the factory's test track at Hamamatsu. A try-out on the bike confirmed what the Japanese technicians were saying. It was a quick bike. Definitely the fastest I had ever ridden and it was no bother knocking a second and a half off the test track record. I was on cloud nine.

The 750 three-cylinder Suzuki was also there to be tried. My long legs didn't really take an instant liking to the bike but with some modifications, I was able to straddle it without too much difficulty. The 750 was a flier too, but I reckoned the 500 was the quickest of the two.

Although I was becoming quite well known on the London social scene and I was beginning to flit about on various business trips, this was the first time I had travelled such a distance. The whole experience was a memorable one and my first look at a way of life strange to mine was really enthralling.

My first pukka works bike! The greatest thrill of the visit was being allowed into Suzuki's secret room where they had this 500-4 ready to be unleashed. I was the first rider ever to be allowed to try it. I felt privileged. But after doing one lap of the test track, I had to stop and think about it because it was so violently fast.

Then, it was much faster than it was when I was to achieve great honours on it more than two years later. The bike had the power band of a 125 and there was a lot more horsepower at the top end then than there was ever to be.

It was just an incredible projectile. Over 150 mph it would zig zag six feet either way up the main straight of the test track if round-profiled tyres were being used. Tyres with a triangular profile made the bike a little easier to control.

It was frightening machine at the time. Along the mile and a half main straight on the test track, the bike would stand up on its back wheel all of the time as it sailed over the gentle rises in fifth gear. Put it into sixth gear and it would rear up again and veer from side to side. It was a real beast that was almost impossible to ride in that state.

In the week we stopped in Japan the technicians did a great deal of work sorting out the power and when it came over for the Grands Prix it was much easier to handle.

Later that year, that same test track was to cause me great worry and anxiety. My career as a racer may have also have ended if that long, fast circuit had been even more cruel to my great friend Gary Nixon.

Gary and I had been buddies since about 1970 when he first came over to England to race. Over the years we kept in pretty regular contact and every time I was in the States we would meet up and have some wild moments.

Gary's reputation in the States was well known. He had been racing for seventeen years on roads and dirt tracks and was still one of the top boys over there. Some of the things he could do on a motorbike, especially on those mile and half mile American dirt tracks, were just out of this world.

Before the Dutch and Belgian Grands Prix in '74, I felt I needed a good team-mate to spearhead the Suzuki challenge in the 500cc classics as a replacement for luckless Paul Smart. Because Gary had always wanted to see what he could do on the European GP circuits and knowing how talented a rider he was, I suggested in a letter to the factory that they should let him race a 500-4 with me. The whole deal was arranged and Gary was really happy about the plan.

Once he got to the test track, chief test rider Ken Araoka began to show him the way round. He eventually encouraged Gary to overtake him and it was after that the 500 seized a piston. Ken Araoka was riding in his slipstream so he had no chance of missing Gary. They say Gary or his bike went 12 feet in the air and knocked the lemons off an overhanging tree.

He was in really bad shape, as was Ken. But I was so cut up about what had happened to my old mate that I gave serious thoughts to quitting racing. If it had not been for me getting Gary fixed up with a 500, the whole sorry incident would not have taken place. Now there he was lying helpless in a hospital bed with his career apparently in tatters. No-one could truly appreciate the grief that I felt during those summer months.

His condition did improve as the months went by and it was indicative of his tremendous spirit that he was back racing in 1975.

That seizure on his Suzuki, which was almost an identical bike to mine, left me short of one hundred per cent confidence with the bike. Would I suffer the same fate?

100

What were the chances of my Suzuki locking at speed? As this was still largely an experimental year for the 500-4's, those questions did crop up in mind from time to time after Gary's accident.

Against that I should emphasise that I never lost enthusiasm in the machine. I knew that it wouldn't be too long before it proved to be a winner. There was no doubt in my mind, as long as we could sort out all the teething problems. All the so-called experts who also thought that I would be unable to handle such a ferocious bike, were of the opinion that the 500-4 was a white elephant, a piece of raceware around for a season and then made obsolete because it could never win.

Well I was dubious about whether the thing would last the race every time we ran it but I was happy enough to persevere. I had faith in the machine and knew that our confidence would be rewarded some day. In fact it took until late summer before me and the bike went under the chequered flag first. That was at the John Player Grand Prix and I'll have to admit the feeling was more of relief than elation when the champagne cork popped that afternoon.

By tradition, the first major meeting of the season is Daytona and this was to be my first stab at the big race. I was going to be in the very best of company and with riders like Ago on the new 700cc Yamaha and Kenny Roberts around, I knew to win this big event would be my greatest achievement to date. There was £10,000 in total prizes at stake, a lot of money for one race which was reduced from 200 miles to 180 because of the petrol crisis which the world was then in.

From the prestige point of view, for both rider and manufacturer, Daytona is an important one to win. But I'd heard all about the sustained high speeds and the strange G-forces caused by the banking and so I was incredibly excited to see what all the fuss was about. First impressions

of the track after taking out the 750cc water-cooled Suzuki
were confused. The sensation of taking the banking at such
fantastic speeds was quite out of this world. It was weird,
almost unreal, as my head was pushed down onto the tank
at certain points because of the effect of the angled
banking. But I was a newcomer to this type of bowl and I
was occasionally sitting up on the bike instead of lying flat
out before I became used to the sensation.

But practice makes perfect and within a few days after
fiddling about with the steering damper and changing to
mag wheels, I was lapping Daytona as quick as those who
had raced there before.

American Number One Kenny Roberts was getting
round in the first private practice session at 106 mph on his
Yamaha 700-4 but I wasn't doing too badly at 105.34 mph!

After the final qualifying round I was fourth fastest
behind Paul Smart on one of the other big Suzukis and the
Yamaha pair of Hideo Kanaya and Roberts, all of us on
107 point something mph. I was even faster than Ago.

What a moment that was for me to be sitting on the
front row of the grid on my 100-plus brake horsepower
Suzuki. But what a terrible start I made. Clutch starts had
never really been a strong point with me and I was thinking
that I did not want to give the clutch too much stick at the
start because I had expected it to be light and fragile. But
there was little likelihood of me burning it out as the
factory had beefed it up, unknown to me. Although I was
well down the order in the early stages, I can remember
coming through, passing one rider after another. Suddenly
I found there was no-one else left to overtake. Roberts,
Ago and company were behind me and I was looking for
Nixon so we could share the glory.

I was leading for a couple of laps but began to be
plagued with ignition problems which forced me out of the
race. The bike was misfiring badly and I thought I may be
out of juice. Then it began to cut out completely before

crackling back into life again and I thought it may have been due to lack of fuel. But it turned out to be a broken ignition wire inside the covering that was at fault.

It was all enjoyment though. The atmosphere was something special and although I would have loved to have won the race, or even finished in the top three, I wasn't too dismayed at my first try there.

My regular mechanic Don had the offer of a good contract that year working in his normal capacity as an electrician and so it was only fair that he should take the job. I couldn't have matched the money anyway. During his absence I took on another spannerman Derek Booth who had been mechanic to Chas Mortimer and had done a bit of racing before. But for the Grands Prix and other international events abroad, I had two Japanese factory mechanics accompanying me.

I was just beginning my driving ban in Britain then but as I was racing for much of the time out of the country, it didn't really bother me. And the £1,000 prize I picked up in winning my opening European international cleared the debts incurred by having to pay the costs of the two-day hearing.

I'd always been respectful of the laws of this country. Not a believer in them but aware they did exist and was mindful of the need to keep the right side of them.

My parents had always taught me right from wrong and so I had never been in any trouble with the police as a youngster. But in 1974, I first saw the inside of a courthouse. It wasn't a pleasant experience. I was at King's Lynn Crown Court as a defendant to answer a charge of driving with more than the permitted level of alcohol in my blood. And another one of dangerous driving.

It started one night after I was taking my friend and Transit Van driver John Blunt in his Capri back from a night out in King's Lynn about ten miles from my newly-acquired home. We'd been drinking at a discotheque. On the way home coming over a hump-back bridge on the correct side of the road, an oncoming car on the wrong side of the road, overtaking a parked vehicle, was in collision with us. The lady driver was unhurt but I had fragmented glass in my eyes from our shattered side window and so I thought the best move was to get home to wash my eyes out. John reckoned my eyes looked like the ends of two sticks of rhubarb at the time.

After that I was going to the hospital for proper treatment and then, because of little damage to either vehicle, intended going to report the accident at the police station. That was the truth and nothing but the truth.

But we were busted by the law. There's no other way to describe it. The police came after me almost at once and they collared me right outside my house. I subsequently failed the breathalyser test. That was an experience in itself not to be recommended to anyone.

But I felt hard done by because I'm sure that proper procedure was not adhered to by the police. I should have been allowed medical treatment before the first breathalyser was administered. I wasn't. And the prosecuting statement in court alleged that the first breathalyser test took place at the hospital which wasn't true.

I had no chance. I was found guilty of the offences and some may say I deserved all I got. Since then, I know I have become very much aware of the importance to stay sober when driving. It just doesn't pay, although that accident wasn't my fault.

My fame as the local road racing hero didn't do too much for my case either. I was fined a few quid but, most galling of all, I lost my driving licence for eighteen months — and was ordered to take another driving test before I could get my licence back. Under the totting up process my two previous endorsements bumped it up to another six months on top of the twelve months disqualification. One of those endorsements was for doing 35 mph in a 30 mph limit and the other for reversing ten feet in my Transit Van on the hard shoulder of a new motorway in Kent. It was the M20 and I was going to see my parents. I couldn't quite take in an unlit road sign and so just edged back to check the directions. I even saw the police car on the motorway bridge spying on me. It was a couple of weeks after the Hutchinson 100 meeting at Brands and, as he booked me, the copper cheerfully remarked: 'Hello Barry, saw you racing at Brands. Pretty good racing.'

Being banned from driving can usually affect people's livelihoods and maybe, as a professional motorcycle racer, I should have pleaded that in court. But, happily, it didn't hamper my activities one little bit. There always seemed to be people around who were willing to drive me about the place. If I was racing abroad dad would drive me to Dover, then I would drive the other side of the Channel, as I did when I contested the big Imola 200 meeting.

John Blunt chauffered me around for much of the time. I didn't mind because I could tolerate his driving. He could drive a car almost as good as I could!

There's no reason to call me a fast driver on the roads. I go quick enough to prevent boredom but I don't take any chances. There's no risk element with me — neither is there on the race tracks — even though I might be cruising at 110 mph on Continental motorways depending on what restrictions are in force.

I also picked up some more money at Imola in '74 for finishing fifth overall but the Suzuki was inferior to the big Yamahas in both top-end acceleration and in weight. Looking at it objectively, I suppose I did the best I could in the circumstances.

If there was one 750cc race that stood out in 1974 it was possibly the fifth race in the John Player Transatlantic Trophy match races between Britain and the United States. Roberts was a knock-out on his first visit to England and he was showing everyone the way round, even though he had never even seen those circuits at all. But I'd seen him operate before and knew he was fantastically brilliant.

The style that made Sheene such a force in 750cc racing during '74.

I also knew Kenny fairly well off the track and one night before Imola we were off out in a hire car along with another American racer Gene Romero. Rent-a-cars always come in for some punishment especially when the Americans get their hands on them. We decided to let Kenny drive with Gene in control of the pedals and me on the handbrake of the Fiat. I'm afraid we were larking about and in our high spirits, the car swerved this way and that alongside a canal before plunging in a somersault down the banking into the murky water.

We were up to our necks in water but Gene, being experienced in that type of accident, had the windows wound down in a flash and he was out as the water began to pour in. One of my legs was caught up under a seat so I had to do some pushing and pulling before I could get out. That left Kenny who was shouting at the top of his voice for help.

We waded through the thick brown, stinking mud and eased Kenny out. When all three of us lay on the bank getting our second wind we all broke into helpless laughter. We didn't care a damn that we all could have been seriously injured, if not drowned. Least of our worries was the rent-a-racer lying almost submerged in the canal.

After a taxi ride back to our rather posh hotel, Gene lay back against the pure white stone wall still laughing at the episode. The manager came out to see what all the fuss was about and he was furious to see this huge brown imprint on his lovely hotel wall in the shape of Romero after he had gone up to his room to change into dry clothes.

But Kenny always took his racing dead seriously and I tried everything I knew to beat him in that incredible race at Oulton Park at Easter, 1974. I finally outbraked him at Old Hall to win but we both kept on setting new lap records. I was quite proud of the fact that I was the only Briton to have beaten him and I became our top points scorer in the process.

But the prize I was gunning for was bigger than anything available in Britain. A world champion, that was my objective and although Phil Read appeared in pretty good form on the 500cc MV Agusta, I felt my Suzuki would give him a fight.

That year I may have been astride the MV alongside Read. It must be every racer's dream to have the opportunity to race MV's. The Italian bike was still a force to be reckoned with in 1974 although wise observers of racing may have begun to see that their useful sporting life in that class was in some jeopardy. While other manufacturers like Yamaha and, more so, Suzuki, were constantly aware of the need to develop their machines, MV looked as if they were sitting back and expecting the same results from the same machinery.

When Count Agusta made the first move to try to get me to sign for MV, I did not dismiss the offer out of hand. The MV magic was then still fairly strong and they had dominated the 500cc world championships for god knows how many years. Only a fool would turn them down. But I knew Suzuki's hopes were high with their 500-4 and I felt I should stick with them. Right from the beginning I had been in on the development of the 500-4 and I had taken a pride in seeing my suggested modifications make the bike perform better and better. It was my project just as much as Suzuki's. They had treated me fairly the season before and I knew they would do the same again for '74. The MV was all ready waiting for me to test ride but I turned the Count down and some time later signed quite happily on the dotted line for Suzuki.

During the moments when Read was winning well on the MV and I was struggling to grab victory on my Suzuki, I did occasionally think what position I might have been in if I had agreed to join the Italian factory. Who knows, I perhaps would have beaten Read for the world title. If I had gone to MV I certainly would have wanted as equally good machinery as Read and knowing of the petty jealousy and squabbling that went on between him and Ago when the two paired up at MV, I didn't want to get involved in that kind of dismal situation. I get a tremendous thrill out of racing and any off-track unhappiness would spoil all the enjoyment.

That's not to say my friendship with Read wasn't a good one. He had helped me quite a lot in my early days of racing abroad and I was grateful for his assistance and, if you like, guidance. With my girlfriend, I had even gone on holiday to Ibiza with Phil and his wife, Madelaine. But I was a big boy then and was well aware of the importance of looking after oneself and one's best interests. It was not a case of not wanting to ride in the same team as Read. I was into a good scene with Suzuki and so there were no further questions that needed to be asked.

But I did manage to have a go on the MV-4 in the Imola paddock that year. As a boy, I looked in awe at these wonderful bikes and always wanted to have a go on one. Well I had a quick flip on it, reckoned it felt great and left it at that. As it turned out they signed up Gianfranco Bonera to partner Read.

But I was super-optimistic about my debut in the 500cc world championships. Brother-in-law Paul Smart would be helping me make a two-pronged attack but I felt at the time that I would have liked an opportunity to have raced the 500 before the opening Grand Prix in France.

It was easy to pick out my rivals. Read, Ago, maybe Lansivuori, even Smartie would be a stiff challenger. But that was about the lot. Not a great deal to fear by any stretch of the imagination.

Smartie, in fact, was nursing a broken arm after his Mallory crash and he did well to go even a lap. So I had it all to do. But I had won there on my last visit and fancied my chances again.

In practice I was three seconds down on Read but

believed I could have topped the leaderboard had not a small stone sneaked into the engine and cracked a piston crown. But with proper factory mechanics working on the machine they soon had the bike sorted out.

Push starting had always been one of my stronger points then. In those split seconds it takes for the flag to drop and the motor to zip into life, I could beat just about anyone.

That's why I knew I'd be about the first to fire at Clermont Ferrand at the start. It stemmed from my early racing days spent as a short circuit man on the Bultacos and Yamahas. There's no need to emphasise the value of being first away ahead of the pack and one of the obvious requirements of quick getaways from dead-engine starts is a sound knowledge of carburation.

I'll go overboard and say I'm the best guy in the country at sorting out and understanding carburation on a two-stroke engine. That statement can be qualified by the low number of seizures I have had. I could often tell when something was not quite right with any bike I was riding and to anticipate mechanical disaster can save a huge amount of time and money. Dad reckoned I acquired this ear for diagnosing trouble by spending so much time in my younger days in his workshop when engines of all description would be running most days.

But I have always had this feeling for two-strokes. The boffins back at the factory in Japan would say that the biggest problem with me was that I knew too much about the bikes. Maybe I did but it's not a bad thing to have sound confidence in the mechanical ability of your engine. And I think the extra mechanical knowledge I possessed gave me an advantage over other two-stroke racers.

When I started to push the bike, I could work the throttle and get the right pick-up. I didn't have to listen for the engine. I could feel it through the handlebars and as soon as it was right, I would be away. There is very little need to use the old conventional bump start technique. As long as the carburation was running fairly rich at low speeds, the engine would pick up revs upon firing and so, with me, it was one step forward and lean over onto the tank so there was enough pressure to make the rear wheel turn the engine over.

That was nearly always my procedure when riding the smaller capacity machine but there was little deviation in my approach to the 500 except that, being heavier, it might take an extra pace or two to push. The moment that engine sparked into life, the throttle was twisted back hard on the stop immediately and I controlled the revs through the clutch lever.

Often I'd get a wheelie on at starts. This happened when I let the clutch fully out to prevent the revs creeping too high but with an advantage already over your rivals, there was time to get the front wheel grounded and still maintain the lead over the pack. Right up until Daytona in 1975, I could be literally guaranteed to be amongst the first away from a dead engine start. Certainly I would be unhappy if I wasn't away in the first five or so.

On this particular day in France, everything clicked. I was first away, and although Read took me on the first corner, I was never too far adrift of the front runners. Ago squeezed by me after a while when I was trying to remove a small insect from my eye. Let Read and Ago settle their differences and see what happens, I thought. My plugs began to oil up after I missed a gear change at the hairpin and, assuming there might be something amiss with the motor, I didn't cane it for a few laps in case it packed up.

But the pit message was clear enough. Bonera, on the other 'fire engine', was catching me and I would have to fly for a bit. Two quick laps must have cleared the engine and I kept a healthy enough distance between my back wheel and Bonera's MV. The extra speed pulled me closer to Read who was leading by then following Ago's retirement with a broken gearbox bearing. He was in my sights towards the end but five seconds difference was too much for me to make up.

Second place on my first ride on the 500-4 Suzuki was way beyond my wildest dreams. The mechanics were happy, the factory was happy and so I went off that evening to celebrate with plenty of French wine in the typical Sheene style in the company of Gary Nixon who flew over specially from the States to sample Grand Prix life.

The bike went well and Suzuki looked to be on the right lines. But after all the excitement died down, there were a few headaches to overcome such as the below-standard suspension and the tendency for the bike to go light at the front. That's why I kept up a succession of wheelies during the closing stages of the race as the fuel tank became lighter and lighter. I know the crowds really appreciated those antics but they weren't entirely intentional. Certainly not at 140 mph in my first 500cc Grand Prix on an untried machine!

King-size wheelies had been one of my trademarks. I know spectators everywhere liked to see them and if I've built up a substantial lead and have the time to spare I'm only too pleased to pop a few wheelies at the appropriate places on the tracks where you're accelerating through the gears over short inclines. The exit from the Mallory hairpin is perhaps the best spot. It's not a case of being a flashy showman. If it keeps the crowd happy, then I'm happy. You've got to entertain as well. Sometimes, of course, wheelies happen naturally without too much over-zealous use of the throttle. Then you really have to be careful.

I couldn't wait to get my six-speed, 90 bhp bullet over the the Nurburgring in West Germany for the next round. I felt that chuffed over the potential shown by the combination of me and the 500-4 that I wanted the next Grand Prix to be held the following day.

But even at the French round, there was talk in the air

about the safety standards that could be expected at Nurburgring. Two years before, there had been undercurrents of discontent over the limited numbers of straw bales lining the armco barriers. What had the organisers done this time? Had they followed the attitude of the French who had complied with our wishes completely over more protection being needed at certain danger points?

We soon found out what measures the Germans had taken when we arrived at the circuit. Precautions were minimal. A trip around the fourteen-mile circuit confirmed our worst fears. There just weren't enough straw bales.

Ago led the protest but every rider to a man, apart from one or two local amateur boys, were right behind him. He even went round with the race chief telling where and how many bales were required and thinking that some action would then be taken, we agreed to take part in the first practice session on the Friday.

It was snowing, it was cold and those were depressing conditions to race a bike in. I dislike the cold on a bike more than anyone and so I had rigged up a couple of lengths of car heater hose which ducted hot air up from the engine into muffs on the bars to keep my hands warm. That was a modification my dad would have been proud of . . . and it worked.

A British rider, Bill Henderson, broke his back when he struck armco in the afternoon and that made us decide we wanted action fast. But the organisers were dragging their heels and the most they thought they could supply was 500 bales when the total should have been nearer 10,000 extra ones.

That night, Ago drew up the now famous petition which we all signed as a protest against the organisers' attitude. Despite meetings with the people concerned and an incredible reaction from the FIM jury present who maintained by six votes to one that the circuit was safe for racing, all the bikes were loaded up and we left the few riders who didn't want to be associated with our protest to get on with it.

It was the first time riders had united in a common cause. We had finally made a stand and the whole world was to know about it. The subsequent inquiry into the events by the FIM found the organisers at fault on both the safety factor aspect and also on their programme on running cars and bikes together at a world championship meeting.

We riders came in for some criticism too, being accused of adopting an 'attitude prejudicial to the interests of the sport and public order'. Well we were not putting our lives on the line for anybody. So we didn't race. The action we took was I'm sure, right, and we'd do it again if faced with the same circumstances.

The tussle was to be resumed at Austria's Salzburgring, although there we had no problems over the question of safety. But it's a funny game racing. In that Austrian round, I finished miles behind in third place and was lapped by the leaders Ago and Bonera into the bargain. But at the end of the race, I was joint championship leader of the 500cc class!

I was going well in practice and was only denied pole position on the grid by Ago going out with no time left to notch the quickest lap. When it came to the big race next day, it was wet and nasty. I was dressed to combat the conditions and in order to keep my hands warm and dry I was wearing washing-up gloves. But I had a stinker of a start, mainly because the Suzuki was not fully warmed up and I had to push the bloody thing for yards before it would fire. Smartie had the same trouble and there we were, on our own, with the pack disappearing at a fast rate of knots.

The ride that day was instantly forgettable. The bike was shod with new hard compound tyres and they were totally unsuitable for the slippery roads. I was skidding this way and that and the worst moment came when the Suzuki went sideways at 130 mph. How I managed to correct the slide I'll never know. Mostly, it was all luck.

I tagged along with my Suzuki team-mate and veteran Australian Jack Findlay and was happy to finish the race intact. Even though Ago and Bonera did come past with nine laps to go, I didn't get too agitated. Maybe a bit embarrassed because I had never been lapped before in the whole of my racing career. Considering the handicap I was under with the wrong tyre on the bike, I was merely glad to pick up ten points for third spot.

A fortnight later, it was the Italian round at Imola and, during training, I was switching first from Michelin to Dunlop, then back again, in order to find the right rear tyre. I was fifth best qualifier.

But even in the race, under dry conditions, I was still sliding about with an old Michelin on the back. It didn't stop me from leading the race after two laps but then Bonera came past and Ago was to follow. The brakes had virtually given up as well at the time of my sudden departure.

What exactly happened after the gear-drive snapped was not too clear at the time. I know before it happened I was thinking I'd settle for third place because of the deficiencies of the machine. Then, bang! I was shooting up the road on my back with the bike in close pursuit. The skin was being rubbed off my shoulders as I flashed over the tarmac. Then I reckon it was the bike that clobbered me and made me see stars. I can recollect Smartie dashing to my assistance and helping others to get my helmet off.

But the next thing I knew I was laying on some couch in an Italian hospital surrounded by nuns in starched white hats and gowns. It was the sheer pain that brought me to. They were scouring my many grazes with what appeared to be scrubbing brushes and pouring on liberal doses of iodine. Did that sting! A bone in my heel was also broken

115

and, most worrying of all, I had haemorraged my right eye and, for a time, the eye would not focus up as it should have done. Eventually it did clear up and the eyesight was perfect from then on. It has been my good fortune that I have not had to wear glasses. A sharp eyesight is an obvious basic for all would-be champions but there have been those guys who have seemed to do just as well wearing spectacles.

My sojourn in that monastic Italian hospital was short and not so sweet and I was soon back in England, foot swathed in bandages to try to retain my King of Brands title for the third successive season. I must have looked quite a sight in my dark glasses and crutches as I was being helped on and off the bikes. The King of Brands title may have gone to Barry Ditchburn that day but I reckon I picked up a few more admirers.

Gary Nixon had his bad crash just before I headed for Assen and the Dutch TT, and his troubles could have had some effect on my racing performance. I had been keen on the plan for him to join me in the Grands Prix but now that was completely out of the question. But his Suzuki's seizure and my last GP prang in Italy made me a cautious man.

And so when the bike began to make an unusual grinding sound on some slow corners and the rear tyre began pattering, I had no hesitation in pulling in. I was up to fifth place and going reasonably well even though the tyres were leading to poor handling. But I didn't want another repeat of the Imola accident so I made my excuses and left.

As far as I was concerned the title was by then a lost cause but that didn't prevent me from trying like the blazes in each GP to beat Read, Ago and Bonera. The Belgian GP at Francorchamps was no exception. There, the bike was motoring nicely and incredibly I managed to knock twelve seconds off my best practice time.

I was even lying second five seconds ahead of Ago and

116

looking fairly secure in that position. But the gear lever came adrift and that was me out again.

Next GP outing was at Anderstorp in Sweden — and my miserable luck continued. Or I should possibly say my good luck started. I would have been clocking 130 mph on a bend just before the start straight on the 500 4 when the water pump seized. I did a handstand on the bike and I was catapulted yards over the catch fencing and Ago followed me. The good fortune that day was that I broke the top of a wooden support post and lived to tell the tale. That would have been curtains there and then if armco barriers had been there instead.

There were no serious injuries, just aggravation of old wounds. Poor Ago damaged his shoulder and that was to cost him the chance of trying to stop Read from winning the 500cc title. But I don't think he held a grudge against me for that. It was something completely out of my hands and I'll go as far as to say that Ago had the time to avoid me. Read and Findlay got past at the moment of ejection and I think Giacomo, panicking, slammed on his front

It can happen to the best of them. Sheene bites the dust at Rouen in France after being jostled at the hairpin. He was unhurt.

brakes in desperation. I was up with the leaders again that afternoon in Sweden before the crash so it was further proof that the bike had the ability to match the opposition machines.

We were then well into August and the season's end was not far off. Still the 500-4 hadn't won and the feeling of some commentators of the sport was that it might not succeed that year.

There was no better place than to get a first placing for the bike than Silverstone. And what a race it was. I couldn't get going at all on it in practice and I left the grid in 32nd position. I had never been so far back for years. But the bike carried me through, despite losing the rear brake on the second lap.

Lansivuori looked as if he might give me a tough time when he pulled out a reasonable lead but he fell back after his gear selector began to give him trouble. I'd taken Read but he came back again on the MV-4. Down Hangar Straight, I outgunned him and let him chase me home. That was it. We had smashed through the win barrier at long last.

The Suzuki 750-3, on which I had set the fastest ever lap in practice at Anderstorp prior to my crash, was quick enough to land me the British Grand Prix laurels and so it was perhaps the most successful meeting of the year for us. The 750 came into its own on the fast Silverstone track and the 106.22 winning average speed speaks for itself.

For some reason I chose to go to contest the final world championship round at Brno in Czechoslovakia, a country I dislike for political reasons, and even with rotten handling and a whole stack of other things going wrong, I somehow managed fourth spot which gave me sixth overall place in the final analysis.

In fact, my best performances in '74 seemed to be reserved for my home crowds and the one I like to think back upon was the Mallory Race of the Year in which I won the

118

loot with Read way behind in my wake and Kenny Roberts blown off, although it was obvious Kenny shouldn't have been on 'wet' tyres.

My personal fame and recognition as a racer was increasing all the time as the '74 season wore on. I was really happy with life in every way although my girl friend Lesley and I parted after a courtship lasting six years. By then our relationship was a dead one. With Derek Booth leaving, Don teamed up as my personal mechanic again.

That win I was searching for in the States still eluded me and both at Talladega and at Ontario I was fourth both times.

When I had sewn up the MCN Superbike series, which was then being regarded as the premier big bike championship in Europe, I felt I had come through a demanding season with credit.

Being the kind of man that I am, it's fair to say I thought I would finish much higher than sixth in the classics but when bikes like the 500-4 and the 750-3 were only really in their infancy as far as development was concerned, my results over the season suggested I was still going up in the world. The financial rewards easily topped anything I had earned in previous season and, for the first time, I had money to spend.

Read took the 'Man of the Year' trophy from me that year. That was only to be expected, him being 500cc world champion but I honestly believed that my following was as great as his. Still I was second in the nationwide poll and a very close second at that, so I was told.

Suzuki in Japan had not been resting on their laurels during the autumn of that year and when I was invited over there to test the raceware they had lined up for the following year, the future looked even healthier. I cannot say it did me much good because I crashed on the test track and knocked myself out but it was plain to see the lighter, more powerful Suzukis would really take some stopping in '75.

119

Suzuki versus MV Agusta. Barry on his 500-4 guns out of the
Mallory hairpin first before Gianfranco Bonera in a 1974 Post
TT race.

The Great Bike Disaster

In any sport where large sums of money can be earned or won, there can be found the occasional out-of-line character who will want to grab his share of the booty the easiest possible way. There have been rough diamonds in motorcycle racing throughout history although shady goings-on have now largely been eliminated.

Gaining unfair advantages over other competitors by the use of illegal equipment became just about impossible with the introduction of tighter scrutineering, and so cases of such irregularities as oversized engines are largely a thing of the past, although gossip-mongers love to make unsubstantiated complaints about allegedly bandit motors when vital world championship points are at stake.

But there are other non-professional aspects of road racing that leave a nasty taste in the mouth. Big money talks in most circles, sporting and non-sporting, and Grands Prix are no exception. But it's all usually cloaked in secrecy.

I can say this now for the first time. In 1975 I was offered a lot of money by a certain individual to let him win an important race. Several thousands of pounds would have been mine if I had allowed this other guy through to win the race. Before the start, he was obviously convinced I would be the danger man.

The laws of libel prevent me from saying any more that might hint or suggest who that person might be but it has to be said that I completely rejected the offer immediately the 'bribe' was made. All my activities surrounding racing

121

have been strictly above board and I certainly wasn't going to become involved in that sort of thing.

Such a proposition made me angry and puzzled me as to why anyone should think I was open to financial inducement to throw a race. The whole business made me go out to win. And win it I did.

If the offer had been a million pounds, I still wouldn't have been interested. I wanted to earn money, sure, but the best way I figured to do that was to win races.

That was the only time I was mixed up with 'non-finish' money. Needless to say, it has never happened again to me.

My racing is for real. I'm paid to do a first-class job and I do it to the best of my ability. Never at any time have I merely ridden comfortably just to earn my start money. That kind of situation is for the dossers. Even as I get older, and perhaps wiser, the thought of just being on the start line to collect a fat purse disgusts me. When the day arrives that I cannot summon up enough enthusiasm or courage to challenge for the spoils, it will be time to pack up racing altogether.

There have been times, especially in the two-leg Formula 750 Championship events, that have proved that I do give my moneysworth. In the Dutch round in Holland, mechanical problems put me out of the first race and there was nothing to gain by appearing in the second leg. But I came out because the fans had paid to see names like me competing, and other top runners often feel the same way as I do about giving good service to the punters.

Organisers, too, deserve fair treatment for the amount of money they frequently shell out and if they are short changed in any way they know how the queue should be formed when it comes around to bargaining time the following year.

The race promoter, Bill France, at Daytona in Florida knows my worth by now. Although they don't pay start money there — which will have to change if the stars of

Europe are to keep going — I have helped to give them world-wide publicity for their meeting.

By the time of Daytona in '75, there had been a big shake-up in the Suzuki America team. Paul Smart had had a wretched season by his standards in '74 and Suzuki did not renew his contract. The same happened to Cliff Carr.

Lansivuori had not had his contract renewed by Yamaha and he was teaming up with me. We would rule as absolute equals. That was good news because I rated Tepi highly. He wasn't too bothered about Yamaha not wanting him. Just the same as I was in '72 although I told them what they could do with their bikes even after I had the chance to renew my contracts for 1973. That bad season I had with Yamaha would certainly affect my feelings if there was ever a time when they were after me to ride their machines again.

Before the Daytona 200 race I had spent some time tyre testing at the Florida track with the 750's and so was becoming rather familiar with the quirks of the circuit.

This was about the first season I started to stay in hotels. I certainly appreciated the comforts of a five-star room with all mod cons compared to a rather cramped caravan with a packet of Cornflakes as a pillow. My off-track merchandising affairs were now being looked after by a go-ahead company and I felt I was at the absolute height of my career.

I suppose I was about hot favourite to win Daytona that year. Roberts and Ago were the very big names, I know, but my initial lap times showed how fast I could go on the Suzuki.

Physically, I was in good shape. My fitness campaign had built up to a peak at Daytona where I was regularly running along the flat golden sands and going with the still-injured Gary Nixon to a local health centre gymnasium. It was hard to recall any other moment in my lifetime when I had been so relaxed and happy. Thames Television were making an hour-long documentary on me and I was enjoying helping the producer Frank Cvitanovich.

My bike was feeling just about right after the factory had made various changes to the frame, steering and motor on my recommendations. Therefore it didn't surprise me that I knocked a couple of seconds off the best time put in up to then by Ago who had won Daytona the year before. It was Roberts I wanted to match. He was lapping the 3.84 mile track in two minutes five seconds and so there was a three-second leeway to make up.

That was well within reach, I reckoned, as I flew round, the throttle right back on the stop and me pinned down over the tank. There was no need to test the bike any further. We knew it was capable of beating the Yamahas.

But in the last opportunity to go out on a private practice session, I wanted to do an authentic 200-mile race to see how both the bike and I would fare under what would almost be race conditions. With my new rear Dunlop tyre well scrubbed in, I dropped the clutch and flew away. Boy, I was moving as sweet as a bird and even on the first lap I was getting around only two seconds slower than the two minutes five seconds I wanted to average at.

By the fifth lap, the tyres were nicely hot and gripping the road perfectly and I must have been clocking 2.5 when I approached the fastest part of the circuit in front of the main grandstand. I had just nicked into sixth gear and had the motor peaking at 8,500 rpm in that top gear. That meant the bike was doing not far short of 180 mph, perhaps around 178 mph, and I was using the full advantage of the dive down the eighteen-degree banking.

Suddenly it happened. The worst experience that could happen to a racing machine travelling at colossal speed did happen. The rear wheel locked solid. One second it had been spinning around at a fantastic number of revolutions per minute, then it was stationary. I immediately grabbed at the clutch lever, but to no effect. The bike had a mind of

124

One more trophy to add to the collection. Crutches by his side Sheene waves to the Brands crowd after receiving the Motor Cycle 'Man of the Year' award in '75.

its own and there was nothing I could possibly do to check its behaviour.

The sensation of the machine swinging sideways in a sudden jerking movement was terrifying. Together we went crazily down the banking and I was projected over the handlebars with maximum velocity.

As I skated down the road on my right-hand side, I was still moving incredibly quickly and I could painfully feel the skin being brutally scraped off my back. Because I retained consciousness all the way through the whole sorry incident, I was also aware of my limbs being battered about and I deliberately tucked my head into my shoulder to try to minimise the possibility of serious neck injuries.

When I came to a standstill, my back felt red raw and there was a lot of blood about. Obviously the rubber back protector helped to reduce the back injuries but there was considerable damage elsewhere, as almost every racing enthusiast knew after reading the papers the next day.

125

I realised I wasn't going to die. That was a fact. But I couldn't see my left leg and I thought it had gone. It was hidden beneath me hideously pointed out sideways to my body. I could also tell my arm and some ribs were broken. Contrary to what some people might have thought, my first concern was not about my private parts. The kidneys were damaged which delayed an operation for a week until the problem cleared up. There was also a fair amount of blood for a time after each visit to the loo. But no, there was no damage to impair my performance in that direction.

I have always said to the people in my team: 'If I crash and I'm knocked unconscious, don't let them cut anything off me.' I never want anything to be amputated. Thankfully, it didn't apply in this accident.

From every other point of view, the crash was a disaster, a major blow to all my big hopes of winning Daytona and more important, of starting off the world championship season.

Sure I was worried about the breakages. But the prospect of being confined to a hospital bed and not being able to get on a bike for months angered me. Just as it all was beginning to look so promising. If there was any good to come out of the crash, then it was the extra publicity I received through the unfortunate accident being shown on television. I'm afraid a lot of people remember me for the Daytona smash-up than for the things I have won.

Anyway, I was carted off the the local hospital and they set to work putting me right. Final tally was a broken left thigh, wrist, forearm, collar-bone, compression fractures of vertebrae and six broken ribs plus a lot of skin missing.

But the doctors, surgeons and medical teams over in the States and in this country worked a near miracle to have me patched up and racing again in seven weeks. There was Claudio Costa, the doctor who did so much for me after my Imola crash in '74 and again this time, a guy in Belgium

and a marvellous chiropractor in Wisbech plus of course
the ones in the Halifax Hospital, a mile from the Daytona
circuit.

They had to cut the tattered leathers from my broken
body when I was admitted to hospital and I later had them
pinned to my office wall at home as a memento. When in
hospital, I was cheered up no end by the 400 get-well-soon
cards from fans in Britain. That was great.

What exactly caused the accident is crystal clear to me. I
have always insisted it was the tyre that had gone after the
tread had come apart from the canvas. The Suzuki
mechanics stripped the machine completely apart to try to
discover if there had been any mechanical fault. They
found nothing wrong.

There had never been any doubt in anyone's mind, Dunlop's included, that the tyre gave up. The actual canvas
shred and just came apart. But who could blame Dunlop?
They weren't to know it could happen. Yet there was

Moment of truth for Barry Sheene as the back tyre explodes at
178mph on the Daytona banking.

another accident two days later on the same tyres and, as the tyre had not been changed at all, I figured the same thing could happen again sooner or later.

OK, so everything went smoothly and there was no repeat of the disaster — until they went back to America with the fast speeds and high temperatures. Then Mick Grant had it happen to him. The circumstances were almost identical. I had been a Dunlop man almost one hundred per cent although I had tried Goodyear on several occasions. So because I could envisage more trouble occurring I switched to Michelin tyres. There was no blaming the Daytona track. That wasn't the fault of my crash and it certainly has not put me off racing there.

Before I was freightlifted back home by plane and helicopter to Walton Highway where the chopper landed in my garden on a big white cross laid out by Frank, loads of people came to see me including Gary Nixon who was lamenting over my fate just as I did nine months before when he had had his freaky accident.

My job was clear-cut once I was home. Get back into a condition adequate enough for racing. That I was out for an incredibly short period was due, as I have said, to great medical care, a lot of encouragement from my parents and such will-power on my own part. I was soon into the press-ups and other strenuous exercises and would carry a hand-grip exerciser around with me wherever I went. But I still needed to have pain-killing jabs every so often and parts of my body resembled a pin cushion.

To ease my blues, I fancied buying a Rolls Royce. Phil Read had one, so why shouldn't I? Even though I was still banned from driving I decided to splash out on the car of my dreams. I'd always liked a Rolls. It was not a case of owning one as a status symbol. I just wanted a car that was a pleasure to drive, looked smart and wouldn't break down too many times.

After all the experiences I had had in the past with vans,

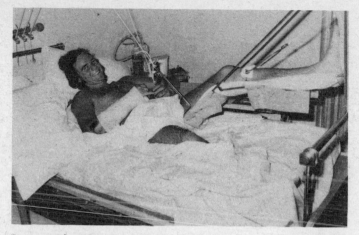

Recuperating in a Daytona hospital bed.

I couldn't stand the hassle of having trouble with vehicles breaking down. My earliest Transit gave me no end of aggravation and there were countless hours spent putting that right when my efforts would have been better used on bike preparation.

After the bother I had with that old van, I made up my mind to get a decent vehicle. With all my savings gone, the new Transit I bought was so much easier, no trouble at all. So, since those days, I have always decided there were two choices: either buy superior machinery or have nothing whatsoever. Any kind of mechanical object should perform almost one hundred per cent efficiently, I reckon, or it's a waste of money.

Everyone knows of the reliability of Rolls Royces, so it was really the only car for me. I had never been struck on sports cars. They were all right to drive for ten minutes but they're not functional. There's a limit on the passenger capacity and, with the size of suitcase I carry around with me to European meetings, I needed something roomy.

In the past, I have owned a Jensen Interceptor 111 but its handling didn't endear it to me. There's also been a V12 Daimler, Mercedes, Ford Granada and a few other wagons. A Rolls was the car I'd always admired. So I had one and later acquired the personalised number plates through friends.

I wasn't really in proper shape when I made my comeback just over a month and a half after Daytona. My left leg with the 18-inch pin neatly inserted in the thigh continued to trouble me and there was difficulty in bending the thing properly. But somehow we adjusted the position of the seat and footrests on the 750cc Suzuki for the meeting at Cadwell Park so that I could ride with as little discomfort as possible.

But I had to go out, I had to race that bike to see if everything was like it was. Daytona was the most frightening thing to ever have happened to me but I was damned determined that it would not have any psychological effect on me racing again. If the crash changed me in some way it perhaps made me a little more carefree, if anything. I had been through the worst, or just about the worst, that racing could be and so any other mishap would have been mild in comparison.

I'd never been afraid of crashing but I didn't go out for a race with the thought of coming off. My riding was not and never will be wild, neither was it chancy. Risks are reduced to a minimum and there's hardly a time when I race on the limit. I ride well within my own capabilities.

But when I returned to the scene at Cadwell Park in Lincolnshire that April, I wasn't worried about whether I could race again. I guessed quite a number of people thought I might be struggling to recapture the same form again and so the quick return at Cadwell was my way of saying: 'See. I'm just like I was.'

I knew it would only take time to put me back with the front runners. That chilly day at Cadwell when I led the race for some distance proved I still had it in me. But I had to pull in after ten laps, because, without a pain-killing jab before the race, I was feeling rough. The point had been made and I was pleased with the way things had gone. At least it scotched all the talk about Suzuki having to get a replacement rider for me!

I am often asked if I believe in luck. Well of course I do. It was only good luck that saved me from death in Daytona. And in other crashes, luck has seen to it that I came off with the least possible damage. When it actually comes to racing and winning events, then I rely very little on luck. Winning and riding well is all down to careful and planned judgement.

I still like to have the gods on my side, though, and that's why I have tended to stick with what I consider to be lucky clothing such as blue underpants and, maybe, a Gary Nixon T-shirt. It occurred to me one day after seeing a picture of me on a victory rostrum that the T-shirt and pants were the same kind I have worn in other races I had won. So I have always kept faith in those garments.

Once, when I came off, I was wearing red underpants, so that colour was out from then on. I wear lots of St. Christophers and good luck charms around my neck all the time to help the cause.

But they didn't do much for me when I went to race in the Austrian Grand Prix that year. Because I was incapacitated, I had been forced to miss the opening 500cc world championship round in France and was desperate to pick up some points. Even though I was still virtually mending, my hopes of getting the world crown were soaring every time I gingerly straddled a bike.

The 500 Suzuki I knew to be a winning machine. My team-mate Tepi Lansivuori had shown in the French race that it was going to give Ago nightmares by leading him until the gearbox packed up.

Even though Suzuki had sent over different bikes from

Japan from the ones I had reckoned on riding, I felt confident of going well in Austria. That was I did until race day. My fitness was improving day by day and my chiropractor was doing a good job on me. He was a kind of osteopath specialising in the manipulative treatments of joints and he was using a machine from which sparks would shoot to burn off the calcium that would build up around the bones.

The new pair of leathers that were cut from Sheene's body following the Daytona disaster.

I was going through the pain barrier every day in an effort to get fully fit and when I tried out a bicycle I had just bought to help regain full knee movement the sheer effort of pedalling at first made tears stream from my eyes.

At a rough estimate, there were around 2,000 cards and letters from well-wishers at that time. Now I wanted to go out in the Austrian GP and show them all what I was made of.

To help restore full movement to my left leg I had also gone across to Belgium for an operation by Doctor Derweduwen who was a wizard on healing the broken bones and twisted joints of moto-cross riders and this resulted in 90-degree movement in the bend.

So I knew I was well enough to make my international come-back. Surely sixth place in practice was sufficient evidence that all was well?

Twice I showed the organisers and FUM officials present that I could push start the machine reasonably well, but I applied for a race pusher and accepted the disadvantage of starting at the back of the field.

But even after dragging me out of my hotel bed at eight in the morning to go for a medical examination to prove my fitness and then examining a favourable report from the Belgian limb expert, the so and so's still felt I was not in the right state of body to race that day. That made me livid. Bang went my chance of gaining valuable points and there was nothing I could do apart from giving the officials a sign to show my disgust.

In the West German round at Hockenheim I fared little better although they did at least allow me to start. So many hours were spent getting the handling and suspension right, we didn't have any time to correctly set up the carburation. The needle and jet settings were not as I would have wanted them when I pushed off from the back of the grid and, after the engine failed to clear on the first lap, a couple of plugs oiled up next time round. I made a pit stop to change them but it was obvious the motor was running too rich when I returned to the fray. It was a hopeless struggle and so I pulled out.

By then, I was well known as the rider with the '7' plate. I asked race organisers for this number even though the number allocated in Grands Prix is the position which you finished in the table the previous season. I first wore '7' at Daytona in 1974.

Seven was always my lucky number and so I wanted to stick with it. Hotel rooms, pits, or whatever, I like them to be either seven or a multiple of seven. Having the same number also makes it easier for spectators to distinguish you at each meeting, especially for newcomers to the sport, and it makes life much simpler by not having to change the plates on the bikes for different events.

And it was the seven bike that Read and Ago saw creeping up on them in the '75 Italian GP. But as I was about to have visions of getting past the pair of them to win, a screw behind the selector came undone and jammed the gearbox. Not only was I out of the race, I was more or less out of the title hunt. Ago was looking set to give Yamaha their first 500cc world championship . . . and I was beginning to realise that some people who were writing to the papers to say I couldn't fully prove myself at 500cc GP level might be right after all.

A few non-championship meetings enabled me to experiment with the 500-4 and to clear up any doubt in my mind that it could be a winner. I beat them all fair and square in Chimay in Belgium and then was confident of repeating the act in the next Grand Prix at Assen in Holland. This was another opportunity to shut up the critics who felt I was making too many excuses for my failings.

My disc-valve Suzuki was running so well before the Dutch TT in '75 and, in practice, I cruised round and took second fastest time. Next session I equalled the best time set by Ago . . . and I was riding round sitting up on the machine. It seemed that easy. Ago, of course, wasn't having any of this and went like a demon to knock three seconds off his previous best lap time. No-one could top that, Yamaha thought.

But I knew my bike was going beautifully and with ten minutes left in the final training spell, I packed cotton wool into a bleeding hole where an impacted wisdom tooth had just been extracted and proceeded to clip a further second of Ago's best. That gave me pole position on the grid — the first time in a GP that that had happened to me during that campaign.

On previous visits to Assen, I had struggled to remember all the various points of the 4.78-mile track and even on this, my third visit, I was still occasionally getting confused. But I was super-confident of winning right from the moment the flag dropped.

The battle was purely and simply between me and Ago after we had dropped Read. His four-cylinder Yamaha against my four-cylinder Suzuki. But I was in complete control of the situation. And I planned on giving the 150,000 crowd their moneysworth.

On a certain part of the circuit through a couple of slow bends I'd make to pass Ago on the right every time. I wanted him to think I'd be coming past on that side, or would try to come past, on the final lap. As we rushed toward the chequered flag, he had his head half-turned waiting for my move through the bend.

But I knew which side I was going — on his left. I'm sure he did not see me rush by until it was too late. I was home first, had fooled the world champion elect and had won my very first 500cc Grand Prix. What a moment to treasure. There were scenes of great jubilation in our camp after the race following my victory celebration lap of wheelies. That was a tremendously exciting day for me. Even more so because I had pushed up the lap record by four seconds.

That made me the only racer in history to have won the

135

50cc, 125cc and 500cc Grands Prix and it will take a long time before anyone emulates that feat. It was a black day for Ago but he had the temperament to get over it. I have always shared a good relationship with the bloke and, although his enjoyment of racing may diminish year by year in my opinion, he's still good for the sport. He has often been attributed with bold, outspoken quotes but the Press have frequently made these appear far more cutting than they really were.

I was bubbling over with joy and thought I could do it all again at the super-fast Francorchamps circuit in the Belgian GP the following weekend. This was MV Agusta's circuit. They seemed to have won there every year since kingdom come mainly because of the machine's top speed suiting that type of circuit. But I had broken the lap record in practice and it looked on for winning number two for Suzuki in the big race.

Speed and power — Sheene and the four-cylinder 500cc Suzuki.

The duel was between Read and me this time. He wouldn't admit it but I had him lined up for the kill with two laps to go. I intended to do to Read what I had done to Ago. We were just coming into the legendary Masta Straight, the quickest stretch of the circuit, and the bike must have been moving at 180 mph.

Then it seized and the Daytona nightmare flashed across my mind. I whipped in the clutch like a flash. I had caught it before it caught me again. I slowed down as the hairs on the back of my neck stopped prickling and then, for some reason, the motor freed itself. I'm not that brave and I let common sense rule on that July afternoon. I was weary of receiving medical treatment, so I cruised back to the paddock. The gearbox was again suspected but it turned out to be a bolt on the drive gear that had sheared.

There couldn't have been a more confident 24-year-old anywhere in Europe as the summer of '75 progressed and the next 500cc round in Sweden was a cakewalk for me. That was an easy victory. The Formula 750 Championship round was also incorporated into the same meeting and although I was beaten into second place by Barry Ditchburn on his Kawasaki in one leg, I took the other race to claim overall victory.

Now the Formula 750 title was still within reach and, in retrospect, I should have perhaps contested the Finnish round instead of sticking to the Hutchinson 100 meeting on the reverse circuit at Brands where I had four wins.

For me the 500cc world championship was over when I was forced out of the two remaining rounds in Finland and Czechoslovakia with mechanical troubles but I had definitely made my mark in this series to make the experts forecast I'd be the ace in the pack the following year.

My chances of winning the Formula 750 award I had first grabbed in 1973 rocketed at Silverstone with my top points score. On paper Johnny Cecotto looked all set to win the overall event until his Yamaha was not fit for the second race. I managed to get Suzuki to loan one of our spares and I did believe in all honesty that this machine was up to scratch. I know there was talk of me letting him ride the spare Suzuki knowing it was a duff bike. But that's all rubbish. I didn't want Johnny to be without a ride when he had a great opportunity to win the top prize and I was as sick, if not highly embarrassed, that the Suzuki died on him especially as he and I were close friends.

Apart from recording my first ever win in Italy in an international at Pesaro and working my way into a commanding position in the Superbike series, there came the lull before the storm. The setting was Mallory.

There were five laps to go in the big £1,500 Race of the Year. I was leading when approaching the Esses which can be a might tricky when there are back markers cruising around.

One jockey was in the centre of the track and it didn't look safe to take him on the outside. So I was about to shoot past him at 100 mph on the inside when he drew in. Being cranked over, I couldn't slam on the brakes so I had to chance my luck by going through. But I was looking what the fool was doing on one side and still had my knee hanging out on the other. Crunch. My knee clattered against the kerb to put me in incredible pain. I still managed to win the race for the second year running, lapping Agostini in the process, but after the finish it was all agony.

My leg felt like it was busted. The leathers all round the knee cap were shredded and now it's obvious why I was later to wear plastic knee protectors which zip into pouches in my leathers.

But apart from some red and blue markings, there looked little wrong with the knee. It felt awful though despite taking a few pills afterwards. I tried the usual thing: forget it and it might go away.

But it continued to give me chronic pain. That week

before the next meeting, an international at Cadwell, a young girl wrote to me saying she hoped I didn't hurt my leg when I banged it at Mallory. Like me, she didn't realise the seriousness of the whole business.

So I went to Cadwell in need of vital points to keep me in the running for the MCN Superbike Championship title. Had there been no urgency about going, I may have stopped at home to rest up the knee.

All my weight, up to then, had deliberately been put on that right leg because I wanted to give the weak left leg as much peace as I could. This put me in a stupid situation. The right leg was now in no form to carry hardly any burden, so the left one, steel pin and all, had to take most of the strain. With the use of blocks on the footrests and the saddle raised, I could navigate the machine with only minor discomfort and I went out to practise on the bike the day before the racing.

When asked nicely to do something, I'm usually willing to oblige whether it's signing an autograph, having my picture taken holding some bloke's girlfriend or having to inspect an out-of-focus photograph of myself taken on a fan's Box Brownie. So there seemed no problem about doing a little wheelie demonstration when a lady asked me.

Ironically it was a Bultaco, the bike I made a start in racing on. I had the front wheel in the air, no trouble. Wheelies had always been a speciality of mine especially when I'm on a trials machine. Anyway, I somehow tipped the bike up too much and when I stepped off it, I collapsed in a heap. The poxy right leg had finally given up and I was left lying there helpless.

An ambulance was called to whisk me off to the local hospital at Louth and the chief medical guy told me I would need an immediate operation there and then. 'You're joking,' I replied. 'If I am going to have an operation, it's going to be in London where I can get the best treatment. My whole career might be at stake.' But he was insistent. 'You've got to stay here,' he snapped. So I replied: 'No way. I'll be off shortly.'

Anyway, I managed to get one of the sisters to find a pair of splints. They were bound onto the right leg and I was carried out to the back of the Rolls. They laid me across the back seat and dad drove the car down that night to the University College Hospital in London.

My confidence in the ability of the people working in London hospitals is far greater than it is in hospitals in the provinces. If they're any good, doctors and surgeons will be working in London where the top money is. And I don't mind admitting I was a private patient. The cost was of no consequence. I just wanted to be right again.

The operation lasted about five hours. Before I was wheeled into the theatre, the doctor reckoned I had only a fifty-fifty chance of having the joint fully operational again. It meant that my future rested upon the skills of those surgeons around that operating table. When he told me that, it just freaked me. My mind was numb. The thought of having all my racing plans come to a sudden and complete standstill did not bear thinking about. I didn't want to be on the scrapheap of racing. I just hadn't realised how serious it all was.

After the operation, the chief surgeon came into my ward and said to me: 'The operation couldn't have gone better. I'm proud of what we have done. The bone inside your leg was just like a hamburger, just crushed up completely.'

I was sore as hell but my spirits were rising after I heard that good news. Then it was a matter of getting through a long period of rehabilitation and a concentrated exercise programme to get the joint knitted into the correct shape.

Right through from October to January, I faithfully attended my physiotherapy sessions for a couple of hours every weekday. Without the terrific help and guidance of my physio Elaine Ranby, who was fantastic all the way through, I would have been sidelined for at least another couple of months. She was brilliant and I have so much to thank that lady for.

Up to the time of falling into her hands, I had hated physiotherapists and had no confidence in them at all. My experiences after the Daytona crash were mainly responsible for having that attitude.

Elaine would make me work my leg, often with the aid of equipment like a stationary bicycle, and she pushed me through a rigorous knee-bending programme as well as administering electrical massage treatment for the muscles. Elaine and the surgeon Ernie Kirwen played the major part in my recovery and they were the people who did so much to get me in good enough shape to race again.

But, for some while, I didn't have a good leg to stand on and it was a twin-crutch job to get about. So, of course the extra pressure on the left leg affected the pin which began to move about and made the thigh swell up. For four days after being released from hospital, I couldn't walk at all and just had to lie in bed.

After I was out of that hospital bed, I knew I'd be racing again soon. There would be nothing that could have possibly stopped me then I thought. The right leg could be bent half-way and I reckoned if that was the full extent of the movement I'd stick the gear-lever up near the crankshaft if it came to it.

I knew I'd be back whatever happened. So every spare moment was spent getting fit. Boy, I really gave my rowing machine some hammer. It worked but I'm still unable to completely bend my knees. I cannot support any weight on my legs. If I get on a high step I have to pull myself up by hand. The right leg will never improve I'm told. It's like that forever. Yet the left will eventually be as good as new after the removal of the nail.

But the right will always be crocked. During the season I don't give it any vigorous exercise in case I strain it. I won't end up a cripple because I take all the steps to prevent the leg seizing up and I go to the chiropractor a lot for electric shock treatment.

The pin didn't restrict my movement in my left leg a great deal, only it bothered me a lot especially if I banged it against a wall. Even laying on it in bed was agony all the time it was in. This rod was due to come out at the end of my 1976 racing calendar.

The right leg that I made a mess of originally at Mallory really gave me a lot of gyp. To cross my legs increased the aches and pains. To stand on it also hurt. There's two screws just below the knee cap which will be there for good.

A lot of people ask to see my right leg because from the knee, it can pivot two inches sideways and it makes a good party piece. It was the worst injury that ever happened to me when the accident finally finished the job at Cadwell in September of 1975. At first, it didn't look like a major setback but it sure turned out to be a wicked one.

What was affected were my dancing habits. A ten-minute shuffle on the fance floor and I had to sit down. Three or four days later, the pain would still be with me.

I could still swim fairly easily but nowhere near as well as I used to. Once, distance appeared no object. At the local swimming baths, three lengths under water was no effort. Forty lengths — not under water! — in a single session was easy going for me. But from 1976 it was only a quiet swim up and down the pool for a few minutes. The activity tended to aggravate the leg. That was a pity because swimming had been a favourite form of relaxation in summer.

Every honour I had a chance of collecting vanished one by one. The Superbike Championship went to Mick Grant, the Formula 750 to Jack Findlay and then, the bolt from the blue, Suzuki Japan announced their major cut-back in world-class bike racing.

What upset me most was having the two big awards snatched from me when there was nothing I could do. With me sidelined it was very much expected that Kawasaki would gobble up the Superbikes but I was hoping for a better effort from the other Suzuki team riders when it came to the final decisive round in West Germany. Findlay did enough to get the points to win with a fourth placing and so that was that. Good luck to him.

Suzuki's withdrawal didn't bother me so much. I knew there would be lots of openings for me and, even if I couldn't earn a works team ride, I had enough money to have formed my own team if I had wanted to. But Suzuki GB's offer was finally a good one and, above all, I would be able to have quality machinery in the form of an even better 500-4. In fact, there was no other bike that would have been competitive alongside the Suzuki and I know that had the bike been reliable all the way through the '75 season, I would have won the 500cc championship and not Ago.

I wasn't worried about not getting works bikes. I knew Suzuki were going to sell their production RG500 racers and I felt totally confident of getting hold of one in some way.

Everything sorted itself out in the end after the financial arrangements with Suzuki GB were finally ironed out. I wasn't at all happy with the original offer made by the British set-up and would have been prepared to have ridden independently if that was their last offer. Damn it, I thought, for the sort of money they were talking about it would be more sensible to ride on my own. Happily, the fee was upped one hell of a lot and so I signed for them.

Away From the Noise

There was nothing special to celebrate that particular winter's night but I had just dined fairly sumptuously in a small, fashionable French restaurant in Knightsbridge and I had a fresh girl hanging on to me. So I was in the mood for a spot of boogeying. I have always been keen on dancing, perhaps because it has always been the easiest and quickest way to meet ladies.

My crocked legs turned me into a bit of a wallflower for quite a few months during 1975 and I can tell you that, of the many things it prevented me from being actively involved in, the inability to get on that dance floor made me even more determined to get back to peak fitness as quickly as was humanly possible. To see my friends bopping around while I sat there helpless was one of the big frustrations of that black year. Besides, I would have hardly cut a dash under the seductive disco lights clattering a couple of walking sticks, would I?

If you're thinking I prey on young females in the flashy night-spots of the capitals of Europe, you're on the wrong track. My so-called heavy social habits are a myth. In the racing season, and that's a long stretch from March to October, I lead a relatively quiet existence in comparison with blokes my age. If I go out during the season, it's always after the racing is over. Like any professional sportsman, the no-drink rule — or alcohol in moderation — the night before the event nearly always applies to me as well. Anyway, I don't profess to be a big drinker — I don't often get tight because I know how rough I can feel the next morning. I used to say I was never affected by booze . . . until the morning after! But, as I say, when there's work to be done and crowds to be entertained and taxmen to be kept happy, I maintain a fairly low profile in the socialising stakes.

Yet when the final meeting is behind me and the pressure and people always around me are forgotten, I do let my hair down just a little. Come winter and I can completely erase from my mind details of race dates, points scored and bike performances.

Then, I don't have to be in a certain place at a certain time, and that pleases me because I have never been keen on keeping to rigid timetables and having to do such and such a thing at a precise time. I've always been a free-wheeler happy to do what I want to do and go where and when I please.

The country house . . .

However, even in circumstances as they are now, I don't have to discipline myself to be punctual, to be polite, be nice to old ladies and young kids and to say the things that are right for all the people involved in my racing set-up.

But again don't misinterpret what I say. I am not a shoot first, ask questions afterwards type. I don't find it in any way difficult being an ambassador, diplomat, call it what you will, for the sport.

I couldn't have wished for a better set of parents and even though this rather stubborn, brash streak has always been part of my character, they brought me up to appreciate right from wrong and bad from good. Maybe I still do have that little bit of cockiness non-Londoners maintain we Cockneys eternally possess.

But I like to consider myself a genuine, honest person and, because of that, I am entitled, just the same as anyone else, to speak my mind on subjects I feel strongly about. Most people I come into contact with are pleasant and friendly towards me and it pleases me that ordinary folks have such respect for me.

I like to reciprocate their friendship. Contrary to what quite a few may think, I am not an arrogant flash boy who has made it to the top and harbours a 'so sod the lot of you' attitude.

It's the race-goers of this world, the people who have forked out some hard-earned cash at the end of the week, who have helped put me to the top of my profession. I have constantly expressed my feelings in the motorcycling Press about my success being largely due to the paying public — and I am not thinking about the start money fees race organisers would be unable to pay out if they did not get those turnstiles clicking merrily.

But for those eight months the pressures can build up incredibly, and when you're constantly involved with trying to pick up world championship points, hoping your bikes are going to stay the distance, and praying like mad you won't bite the tarmac at speed, the tension and worry can reach boiling point. Matters aren't helped either with the thought of how much money is at stake and how much can be won and lost in future seasons.

So passing under the final chequered flag of the year is now for me an occasion of tremendous relief. My racing commitments are over for a while and I can cruise around to my heart's content. My phone will still be ringing every two minutes but at least I will have a respite from the back-slappers and well-wishers, as welcome as they are.

After one Post-TT meeting at Mallory Park, I was besieged in my caravan. It seemed half the 40,000 crowd had stayed on long after the last race in the hope of getting my autograph. Normally, I'm happy to sign anything for fans, pictures, T-shirts, plaster casts, parts of people's bodies. But on this occasion, I was marooned in a sea of pen-waving hands and arms. I could see the side of the caravan by the door would be pushed in sooner or later and there were young children on the point of being crushed and trampled on as the crowd became tighter. We were having to pass small boys through the windows to prevent them from being hurt.

If I had casually ambled out, maybe I might have had my clothes torn off me like a scene from one of those pop concert hysteria films. I should be so lucky! Anyway, my girlfriend and I made a super-quick dash to the Rolls and we escaped unscathed.

But repeat the same kind of incident between events on each race-day throughout the season and you can imagine why I am reluctant to let anything interfere with my privacy and 'holiday' time from November onwards.

It brings me back to that particular evening again when I was escorting this lovely little blonde. Her name was Jane, I think. As is usually the case when I am in London during the winter, I lay low during the daylight hours often involving myself in some of my business interests and zoom off into the big bad world when the sun goes down.

Well, one of my nocturnal habits, when I am ready for a spot of dancing, is to head for Tramp. Controversial 'gossip page' journalists such as Nigel Dempster of the *Daily Mail* like to call it London's 'most fashionable watering-hole'. It's a very pleasant discotheque/restaurant nightspot where you can dance, drink or dine until about five in the morning. It lies in Jermyn Street just off Trafalgar Square and one nice thing about the place is that you can leave the Rolls in the narrow one-way street outside the swishy front doot and a uniformed commissionaire will whisk it away, to some nearby car park. At least that's what I think he does with it. He may go for a joy ride in it for all I know. Anyway, it is always being driven round to the door when I'm ready to go which is always well before kicking out time.

Tramp attracts a wide variety of people in the public eye, especially those involved in the pop music and film world. I've seen dozens of big names there in the company of others who are unlikely to be husbands, wives, fiances or what have you. That's why the gossip columnists like to home in on the place.

I've come under scrutiny by these hawkeyes in the past, the last time before my little thing with Stephanie McLean became public knowledge was when I was seen out and about with Pammie Townley, a dark-haired model who was the daughter of an admiral, I think.

Although only a regular visitor when staying in town, I patronise this club because it offers anonymity. There's no chance of being overwhelmed or being bothered by people. It's worth £30 a year. The membership list closed years ago and I did hear rumours that the club might possibly pack up.

Going back this evening under the dim chandeliers of Tramp's basement disco, I was also in the convivial company of Lord Hesketh who tried so hard to produce a winning British racing car, and Frank Cvitanovich who makes great films for Thames Television. He compiled the one on me in '75 which was screened nation-wide and showed my demon Daytona crash that nearly put a stop to it all.

In Tramp, swarthy men in white polo-neck jerseys come out of the gloom at you, lighter in hand, like fire-flies, when you pull out a cigarette. Certainly there's no need for the Swan Vestas.

As a Diana Ross song flooded the room with gentle sounds and the rest of my party chatted, I sat back and tried to get the whole purpose of my life as a motorcycle racer into proper perspective.

I had been in the racing wilderness for four months following the rather freak accident at Mallory Park. I earned £1,500 in prize money for winning that race but it cost me so much more than that, both financially and mentally, in the long run. My right leg was in dock and my left was still a long way from being fully usable after the mess it was left in from my 178 mph slide at Daytona.

So there I sat — two wobbly legs away from the 500cc world championship. If I had been fully fit in '75, I believe I could have won it. In the proper shape, I knew I could do it in '76. My bikes would be good enough if they behaved. It was now up to me.

Despite my run of ill-fortune with injuries, I knew I had it in me to beat my rivals and yet, pressure on me was growing all the time to finally prove to the doubting Thomases that I was a world star. You can win all the big money races in the world but until you've collected a world championship medal from the FIM, you're not truly in the superstar bracket.

Second place in the 125cc class was the nearest I had been to that coveted world championship dream. That was back in 1971 and a few non-professional critics were beginning to ask when I would produce the goods.

Although my bank balance was extremely healthy at that time and I was being allowed to pilot the fastest racing hardware in the world, I knew 1976 must be the year when the hopes and dreams I had cherished for so long would come true.

I would be 26 that year and the realisation that teenagers were beginning to make it hot for me out on the tracks of Europe spurred me on even more to bring bike racing's most prestigious prize back to Britain again.

It's an old saying that you can achieve nothing if you have no belief in your ability. Well I had 100 per cent confidence in myself especially on the super 'works' Suzukis. But I place a greater emphasis on skill and determination rather than the capabilities of machinery — and I reckoned I was as good as any rider in action at the time.

Barry and his girl Stephanie.

The Greatest Year

I have always found it somewhat hard to change my outlook. A devil-may-care attitude has prevailed throughout my life and I daresay I will continue to approach most problems without too many worrying thoughts buzzing round my head.

My carefree nature has brought me a satisfying life so far and I see no reason to depart from that course. But possibly the biggest change in my personality came during the beginning of 1976. It will always be remembered for the time I stopped being a motorcycle racing stud and learned the real meaning of love.

My reputation has often preceded me. As far as women went, I was the man for all seasons. A different girl each night was my regular pattern . . . if there was enough energy for the next day. There were even weeks during that winter when I would be saying goodbye to one young lady, immediately chatting another up on the 'phone and eyeing the clock to see how soon the third would be arriving. Up until my late teens, the most I would share my bed with was a copy of *Motor Cycle News*. Now it was all happening to me. I still think they should have made a sequel to 'Confessions of a Window Cleaner' and called it 'Confessions of a Bike Racer'. I would have taken the leading role, of course.

Publicity as a racer undoubtedly caused me to be recognised whenever I was relaxing in restaurants, nightspots or wherever and for that reason there was never a problem over introductions. Dishy ladies would come up to me and say: 'I saw you on the television. You race motorcycles don't you?' It was all so easy, and even the crutches and walking sticks that I needed to get about during those winter months failed to put them off.

George Best used to be the sportsman to beat all sportsmen for pulling the birds. Well I can tell him he had a serious rival in that field. My habits with members of the opposite sex remained almost unchanged from the first time I went abroad as a rookie mechanic right through until the 75/76 winter. The only exception was the one real lasting friendship I had with Lesley who I saw one day in the street, fancied and chatted her up. I was seventeen at the time.

But we drifted apart and I began to discover that a lot of females wanted to be seen with Barry Sheene. But it was just as much a case of me using them as much as them using my name to boost their egos.

Things got worse, or better, depending how you view it, when Piers Forester offered me a room in his town house after I had had my knee operation in the autumn of '75. He would often visit me in hospital after we had first met at a Bemsee dinner, and his way-out humour lifted my flagging spirits. When I was about to be discharged I wanted to base myself in London during the winter so, with nowhere else to go, I reckoned on staying in a hotel until I was fully mobile again.

But Piers' invitation seemed too good to miss and I can honestly say he played a vital part in my comeback. There were so many things we got up to at his place but, unfortunately, most is unprintable. Piers would receive scores of invitations to what we called 'headscarf' parties. They were, in fact, gentle cocktail parties given by ladies of London society where you sipped gin quietly, smashed your way through trays of little things on sticks and seemed to have to talk in snooty loud voices.

Piers would always make me go along. He was OK because his Old Harrovian accent was refined enough to blend in with the general conversation. My dialogue is

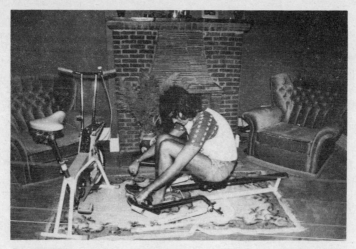

One man's way of keeping fit.

genuine mint Cockney so I was a bit like a fish out of water.

But our plan was to get as many laughs out of those cocktail parties as we could by taking a rise out of their high-class behaviour. At the conclusion of those *soirees*, Piers and I would both go off with a Lady so-and-so or the daughter of a Lord somebody.

But it was while I was staying at Piers' place that I first came into contact with Stephanie McLean. It was eventually to lead me to say: 'That's the end of this different girl every night stuff.' The long line of models and affluent young ladies was to come to an end. One of my escorts had been a millionaire's daughter. Perhaps I could have set up my own racing team sooner if I had stopped with her.

Stephanie and I first came together one night at Tramp, the club where I loved to go. She reckoned the lights flashed momentarily on my left crutch and it caught her

153

eye. I tell her it was my good looks that did it. Steph had noticed my colourful red, white and blue racing leathers in the Daytona TV film and she thought they would make an excellent modelling costume for her. The way it worked out was that she did look a wow in my suit and it was to lead to us getting together. About then, I remember her coming into the house to show me her Christmas shopping and another bird just happened to be coming downstairs. The thoughts that must have been racing through her mind!

The fact that she was married at the time to a well-known London fashion photographer did not help to make the course of true love run too smoothly. And when she came over to stay with me for the first time prior to the French Grand Prix, she had diarrhoea for a week which makes it all sound rather less romantic. I had to curb my natural instincts as well and I don't think she was too keen on my early behaviour when I shot my hand up her jumper. But I've quietened down now.

It didn't come as a surprise when we heard our relationship had made the national papers but we didn't think it was worth the big front page treatment in *The Sun*. First time we became aware of the publicity was when a reporter from that paper caught up with us at Salzburg and showed us the news. We had nothing to hide so we just about revealed all. Pity in a way really that I couldn't earn as many column inches for riding a bike. But we were relieved it was finally all out in the open. Steph was not unused to all this page one and page three treatment. Her modelling career had given her wide exposure and she had done stacks of assignments for all the big brand name products. Steph, or Booze I call her, because I have noticed her liking for wine, spent many years of her childhood in Malaya where her father was a warrant officer in the Army.

When her family came home, they settled in Chester and she went to Lucy Clayton's modelling school before moving down to London. Steph worked as one of those bunnies in the Playboy Club, all ears and tail, but she didn't like the job and she really got into modelling work after she married Clive and had her lad, Roman.

Now, I'm not a bit interested in anyone else. She has completed my happiness. People said it was not in keeping with my character but it proved that I have settled down and changed from what I used to be like. Before I'd go charging around the paddocks at a Grand Prix hoping to fix up with some girl. I seemed to have to be seen to be doing that. But all that's in the past and I couldn't give a monkeys about the bachelor playboy image being ruined. The image was only there because that was what I was like.

Our friendship was beginning to blossom when I went out to Japan in the late winter of '76 to have final test rides on the so-called *special* RG500 four-cylinder jobs that Suzuki had modified for me. They went well but there was nothing to shout about. When I went round the test track on the production RG500 I was lapping at only half a second slower, so, in a way, their development work hadn't been shattering.

Some newspaper reports said I broke one or two of the engines during those tests because I was taking them over the limit. That wasn't true. All I did smash was one of the front disc brakes. The machines looked pretty sound, anyway, and I was confident that if they were to prove solid and reliable throughout the season, I would collect the 500cc world championship.

But the first major task of the season, and a severe test of what my battered body would stand up to, was Daytona. Two hundred miles of mind-blowing speed on a circuit that had dealt me a crushing blow the year before. I had no dislike of the Florida track. I wasn't frightened to any great extent. If the bike behaved itself this time, there was no reason why there should be anything to get unduly alarmed about.

The days leading up to Daytona were quiet by my standards. Stephanie wrote to me almost every day and she often phoned. I think I wrote four letters back. In the evenings, I'd stay in and talk with friends or watch TV in my room which was a complete contrast to the activities I used to get involved in. Stephanie had had a dramatic effect on me! It hadn't done anything, though, to quieten my determination to go out on a bike and race. All the old enthusiasm was there. It was just that my body wasn't quite ready for all the excitement. I had still never won a race in America and I was keen to do so. For a Briton, or any European for that matter, to win in the States is a fine achievement. It was a big ambition with me.

I'd occasionally go out with Gary Nixon, my old mate, and we'd go dancing, do some drinking and generally have a good time. I was going easier on the shorts then. During the winter when I was at home I was drinking so much red wine I would often come out in a nettle-type rash. By going out to dinner most evenings, I must have been averaging a bottle a day without really thinking about it. The intake had to be reduced, the doctor said, and I switched to white wine because it seemed lighter. The rash went completely. Vodka was also taking the place of brandy as my other favourite drink although I'd only have that in small quantities.

But, with Daytona, I knew I had precious little chance of winning it on my 750cc Suzuki. But I wanted the opportunity to see if I could get back into the groove once more.

My Suzuki was just so slow compared to the Yamahas and I finished a disastrous thirteenth fastest qualifier in practice, almost five mph slower than Kenny Roberts who was in pole position.

The right leg was playing up and giving me rotten pain. Movement was a bit of a problem and team manager Merv Wright built some three-inch blocks on the saddle of the bike to make it more comfortable. It was not the previous operation that was at fault, but a strain of the ligaments and muscles.

To get away off that grid amidst all the incredible noise almost masked the agony I was in. I was pleased to be racing once more. And I think I did fantastically well to get into second position behind Cecotto before the chain jumped the rear sprocket, jammed round the swinging arm and locked the back wheel. My annoyance at going out to something as simple as a busted chain was expressed by the dent I gave the fuel tank with my fist. My anger subsided later when it dawned on me I had achieved a personal victory by overcoming a physical deficiency and my rivals superior machinery. Certainly I had done enough to prove to myself that I could ride again, and ride well at that.

Among the obstacles that had to be surmounted in 1976 was the business of push starts. My legs rebelled against any undue physical pressure such as heaving a heavyweight motorcycle and I realised if I didn't get the bike to fire almost straight away, I would be struggling. It was difficult pushing it in every Grand Prix because I could never get into a quick sprint with my limp. I should say I made only one decent start in all of the 1976 GP's and that was in the Belgian. But that was only because the start line was facing downhill.

In the opening round at Le Mans in France, Frank and Iris, Stephanie and my van driver John and his girl friend Angie were all willing the machine to burst into life when the flag went down. I gave my instructions to John before the start. I said: 'If it doesn't go, jump over the fence and push me like hell. I don't care who you have to smack in the teeth to get over, just do it.' Fortunately, it went first time although I was left behind by most of the pack. John was a little worried about the orders I had given him because there was a rather unfriendly-looking gendarme positioned right in front of him. But I'm sure he would have pushed through to help me. We Fenmen stick together!

Now I would like to see push starts abolished completely. Spectators are accustomed to clutch starts these days and it makes for a lot closer racing. In all classes, it can get everyone away at the same time. I'm not saying that because of my legs. They're not much of a disadvantage when starting. I'm just thinking of how the sport could be improved. Another way to encourage a clean, fair start is by using the traffic light system instead of the traditional flag held by someone standing on a box.

But it should be three lights instead of two. The red light should go on with three minutes left and then the yellow light at ten seconds to blast off. For only ten seconds, there are going to be few burnt-out clutches. Engaging gear for any longer than ten seconds can often lead to ruined clutches.

As far safety is concerned, racing is getting a lot better. And organisers are doing as much as they can to keep bike racers happy. Obviously I'd like to see armco barriers completely replaced, banking moved back and catch fences erected. But it's all steadily happening.

Another personal hope which could improve racing is to see people elected to the FIM who are go-ahead and who understand the sport and the riders. They should also be businessmen interested in the betterment of racing. Grands Prix, as they stand, are an utter financial disaster for racers. Nine cases out of ten, GP's lead to nice big lumps in the pockets of the promoters.

When I began the world championship programme at Le Mans in France I was in no doubt I would win the title provided the bike did not strike trouble. No-one could tell me any different. I also knew I could ride at least as fast as everyone else who was contesting the 500cc class.

Before the opening round, I feared one man might get in the way of my hopes. That was Johnny Cecotto. The year

Bring out the bubbly.

before he had shown how smooth, yet how quick, he could ride and we had had some good dices between ourselves on 750's. He was to be mounted on a 500cc works Yamaha and we weren't entirely sure what it was capable of.

When Johnny crashed in practice twice and could only make third fastest qualifier, I tended to put the Italian Marco Lucchinelli at the top of the list of the men to be wary of. I had seen him operate at Imola earlier in the year and I knew he could be a threat. His training time was only fractionally slower than mine which was achieved on Dunlop slick tyres. It was the first time since Cadwell in my '75 come-back ride that I had used Dunlops which did enable me to go quicker at the Bugatti circuit than on Michelins.

I wasn't afraid of either Ago or Read although I realised Phil would make life difficult for me at some time or another. You don't keep going as fast as he has done for twenty years and still not offer a stern challenge.

I would have preferred to have used a pusher that day but the FIM turned me down, so it was heave-ho and finally away. Eventually I saw there was only Cecotto between me and the lead. I waited a few laps to see how he shaped up on certain bends and he kept waving his hand at me to tell me to keep away. When I outbraked him at one point to head the field I gave him signals to encourage him to overtake me. But I decided to open a useful lead and that was that.

One down, perhaps only another five to go. Ago maybe knew then the situation looked gloomy if he wanted to keep his 500cc title. But I don't think he cared one way or the other. After his MV proved unreliable and he had his first few rides on his newly-acquired Suzuki he'd say: 'Suzuki give nothing but trouble.' I'd reply: 'You're revving the motor too hard, that's why you're breaking the con-rods. It won't stand a load of stick.' But Ago was to tell an Italian newspaper reporter much later that I fully deserved to become the new world champion which was a kind of nice thing for him to say.

But after the French opener I was prepared for the comments about me having it easier than the others just because I had a works bike. There would always be some excuse so I accepted I would be knocked like that even before the season started.

The next confrontation at the Salzburgring in Austria turned out to be the easist Grand Prix of the lot. It was forty-three laps which, although I don't like long races, pleased me because I could go just as fast at the end of such a long race as I had done at the start. A lot of riders go quick at the beginning, quick half-way through and, at the end, go slowly, through tiredness usually.

It's no use having a short fuse in lengthy races. Maintaining the same pace is very important although I like to have the easiest ride possible.

I got through to the front at around three-quarters distance on my new machine in Austria, and stuck there ahead of Lucchinelli and Read. Five years before, I was just about on racing's breadline when I first went to that Austrian track. In '76, I was able to check into a magnificent hotel which had views over the snow-covered mountains. Before, it was the inside of a van sited in a spartan paddock.

Before going off to Mugello for the Italian GP, I had a great dust-up with Mick Grant at Cadwell in the Superbike series and I really had to put the hammer down to get past his Kawasaki. It was beginning to occur to me that my Suzuki 750-3 was slowly becoming less and less competitive alongside the Kawasakis when the 'green meanies' were on full gas.

Mugello was a horrible circuit. Like Le Mans, it was my first race there and the only way I would return would be to race in a GP if any more were held at that terrible place. When I was invited to compete there in an international meeting at the end of '76, I immediately rejected their huge offer. It was definitely the circuit I rate as the one I like least of all. There were lots of tiny ripples on the track surface and every one of the dozens of boring second corners appeared the same. It was both uninteresting and dangerous.

But that race involved me in my closest finish of the season. When I raised my arm in salute across the finish line with Read just half a machine's length adrift, I knew precisely what I was doing.

Earlier in the race I had sussed out where I could make up ground on Read and I felt undisturbed about letting him lead. But I headed him as we approached for the final corner where braking tactics had to be called for. I braked a little early to let Read through on the inside, an opening he accepted. But it left him four feet further over than he should have been. That was perfect. So I went out and took a wide swoop in and a tight swoop out. I was under the screen going flat out while he was still on the corner.

That was tactics working out just right. But I have to say this about Phil. Of all the riders in all the classes I have faced, he has always been the most difficult one to beat. Although 1976 saw him almost certainly coming to the end of his career, Readie was the man who would always keep coming back and was never easy to shake off. He just never would give up in the 500cc Grands Prix.

But that Italian win meant that I had three in the bag and I knew it would take something really big to stop me. In the next round at Assen in Holland, I was almost beaten — by the sweltering 100 degree heat. That was the hottest day's racing of my life and, at one stage, I reckoned I'd expire in the exhausting conditions. My greatest battle was against fatigue and it was obvious all the physical exercises I continued to do helped me stand up to the mind-bending weather. After a poor start, I managed to gobble up both Read and Ago by outbraking them to make it four GP's in

His body disappears under a volume of silverware and laurels after winning the Italian Grand Prix at Mugello.

a row. The first thing I did after winning that grueller was to tip a bucket of water over myself. Talk about being revived in the nick of time!

Those hot conditions seemed to make all the pain from the old injuries re-awaken. And when you race a 500cc or 750cc machine, you know at the end what it's like to be really tired. The body aches and the mind goes slightly numb after a tough race. For me, the heat tends to aggravate the situation even further.

Everyone reckoned I had the title in my pocket after the Dutch TT but I needed to be convinced. Ago told me if I won the Dutch, I had the championship sewn up. And the pressure was building up on me to win. So I tried extra hard to win that race. But the worst thing I can ever experience is to go to a meeting where there is no competition. Of course, that hardly ever happened much after '75.

When the news broke that Read had left for home on the eve of the Belgian Grand Prix because of a domestic problem, I was slightly disappointed because I wanted to beat him at Francorchamps after I had had him lined up in my sights the previous season. But this could have been the round where the world title could finally be clinched. A win by me and low placings for men like Lucchinelli and John Williams would have settled the issue once and for all. The way it turned out, I was extremely fortunate to pick up twelve points for second place behind Williams. The 500-4 was displaying its first signs of trouble in public and it was only luck that allowed me to reach the chequered flag after the bike had been struck with fuel vapourisation in the heat of the 170 mph race.

At about that time, there was an incident that took place many miles from a race track that could have undone all the good work my team and I had put in during the year. It could have ruled me out of the Swedish round and maybe the others as well.

One evening in July, I was dining in Wisbech with friends when a waiter tapped me on the shoulder and told me someone was trying to break into the Rolls Royce parked out through the door in a quiet street. I rushed outside and saw three guys around the car. Two walked away when they saw me come out but the third, who was about twenty stone and six feet high, kept trying the door handles.

'What's your game?' I asked.

'Mind your own business, I'm trying to break into this car,' he snapped back.

So I replied: 'Well that car happens to be mine. Clear off and leave it alone.'

He shouted back: 'No I won't. Who do you think you are parking on the pavement?'

So I asked: 'What are you, a traffic warden?' This geyser got nastier and nastier and he began to call me four-lettered things. I'm quite a tough guy when I get roused and I was all prepared to smack him in the teeth. But judging by his size, he could have mangled me up and put me out of racing for a while.

One of the other blokes come on strong with the old line 'Just because you've got a Rolls, think you own the place.'

So I said: 'If you didn't spend your money getting drunk, you might have something of your own.' It was true, because if anyone can get their act shaped they can make a success of life. Well I wanted the big chap to apologise for calling me unmentionable names. It took me three times to ask him to say he was sorry and I was all prepared to hit him. The third time of asking, he did apologise.

A trophy worth keeping! The magnificent Mellano Trophy, won for a third time in '76 by Sheene, is displayed by a proud father to former Suzuki GB team manager Rex White.

The Dream Comes True

They say some professional footballers don't always give one hundred per cent effort in certain matches if their team has a Cup Final date looming up. They don't want to miss the big day through injury. Well I could have adopted that attitude during the whole of my 1976 world championship campaign by only riding in Grands Prix, until I was certain of the title, and skipping all other meetings.

It wouldn't have meant me earning a lot of money but I could have kept myself wrapped in cotton wool and reduced the risk of injury that would keep me out of the vital rounds. But that's not my style. I live to race and it's very easy to become complacent about riding after a lengthy lay-off.

Before the most crucial outing of my life in Sweden, I chose to head not many miles from my home into the wilds of Norfolk for a good class-entry meeting at Snetterton. I hadn't been there for a few years and I fancied a run-out to ensure the machines were in tip-top condition for the next Grand Prix.

But when I zoomed off the circuit at great speed while in pursuit of Mick Grant, I wondered if I had made the right decision to race there with the world title still in the balance. I hurtled into the banking and went end over end. Sheer luck prevented it from being a bloody major spill and all I could boast after I had been extracted from the ambulance was some heavy bruising. It was all caused, unbelievably, by the front brake pads falling out. I felt decidedly secondhand, so Stephanie had to chauffeur me home that night.

167

But I was looking more like my normal self by the time we arrived in Sweden for the sixth round of the classics at Anderstorp — the venue where all my hopes and dreams of three years could come true.

The machines were the big worry. My number one bike had to be rebuilt after the Snetterton mishap and when we unloaded the transporter in the paddock in Sweden, we noticed there were the wrong triple fork clamps on that machine. There were other problems too — we had no record of the right pressures to use in the air forks and my number two bike had been given the wrong gearbox.

It was difficult to lay the blame at anyone's feet but somewhere there had been a right cock-up. Don and Franco weren't at fault; it was a case of being sent the wrong parts from the stores at Croydon. Michelin had also sent me the wrong tyres.

I practised on really old tyres that I had previously used at both the Belgian Grand Prix and at Snetterton and managed to get fastest time in the first practice session. All seemed well.

In the second session the next day, I caught John Williams up on his 500-4 Suzuki and was interested to see if there was any difference in our bikes. He wasn't used to riding Michelins and couldn't have been aware that the tyres were still cold. They take a long time to heat up. We were only on our second lap and he screwed it on too hard at this particular corner and hit the ground really hard.

I helped him the best I could, clearing away the dirt and grass that seemed to be blocking his air passage. I rode back to the pits to explain what had happened but, with laying the bike down to see to John, the plugs had oiled. After they had been changed, I had just sped out on the track once more on the spare bike and the head gasket blew. So one lap and I was back to have another try on the number one machine. But the plugs oiled again and when I had another go and before we knew it, practice was over and I was way down in fifteenth position on times for that session. We did manage to discover that the choke cables were round the wrong side of the steering head so all the chokes were pulled out, drowning the engine, every time the handlebars were turned.

Tepi Lansivuori, riding so well then, put up the quickest time in overall practice but I was optimistic about gaining the best lap time in the second session until the gremlins struck. I had really intended to put the hammer down at the final attempt.

Fortunately, Tepi hadn't enough points to catch me in the title race. I rate him as the best Grand Prix rider around and he is an extremely hard man to beat. He has just had so much bad luck with bikes.

With the best six placings only counting in the final analysis before the FIM thought about changing the system later in the season, I was sitting pretty with 72 points. Because of his win in Belgium, John Williams was one of only two men who could still pip me. But now he was laying in a hospital bed away from the action, a situation I had experienced on many occasions. Marco Lucchinelli was really in a stronger position because he had a second and a third to make up his 22 points while John had three scores for his 24 points. If Lucchinelli had won all the remaining four rounds and I had finished third in Sweden, we would have been tying on points at the end of the series. We would both have had four wins, plus a second and a third place.

Funny thing was, though, I was keeping a close eye on 'Lucky's' practice times even after I had shown him the right racing lines to take as it was his first time at Anderstorp. He's a good, talented young rider who can only get better with each season. In Italy, 'Lucky' is big and is definitely one to look out for.

I wasn't nervous at all about the task that lay before me. My only doubt surrounded the reliability of the bike and whether it might break down. I was also slightly worried about starting the race with brand new tyres. The first four laps would have to be taken fairly slowly to get them scrubbed in.

After reading the good luck telegrams I received at my hotel, of which one was from the girls at The Auto Cycle Union offices in London — not the hierarchy, just the girls — I arrived at the circuit in time to watch the 125cc and 250cc races and to down a few cups of tea. I was then ready for my contest.

On the starting grid I was again looking happy and was generally having a laugh. Some people think that that is my way to try to psych out my rivals because any natural pose at that key moment should be one of seriousness. Not a bit of it. Usually there are riders beside me who will share a joke, even at the tense moment 'the ten seconds to go' board is held up. Next to me in Sweden, was the Swiss rider, Philippe Coulon, and Tepi Lansivuori, the man I felt would make it tough for me. I was trying to take the mickey out of Tepi as the final countdown approached but he'd twiddle his blond moustache and confidently say: 'No problem for me today.'

The wife of a guy from the Swedish Motorcycle Federation was nearby with her smashing little baby, a beautiful boy I hadn't seen for a couple of years. So, just before the flag was raised, I was waving at this little lad and he was waving back.

I don't need to put on a front purposely, it's a natural reaction. It's a cover-up for nerves. What is there to be nervous about? Whatever is going to happen is going to happen. No-one can decide fate. I know I have had lots of misfortunes in previous years so that should be even more reason not to be nervous.

At the beginning of the year, I'd think: 'There's no way I'm going to win the 500cc title. Something's going to go up the pictures to prevent me from doing it.' So I accepted the fact that something was going to go wrong. But I also knew that if nothing went wrong with the bike I'd win the championship.

I was sure I would win the world championship that day if the bike didn't break down. But if I had found it really difficult to beat Tepi I would have settled for second place.

The number one bike's plug problems had all been sorted out and it was to run like a dream. But I made a bad start, as did Tepi, but he went past and pulled out a four-second lead on me on the second lap. It was a great temptation to go after him but I had my work to do in scrubbing in the new tyres.

Knowing there are twenty-eight laps, there was enough time to catch Tepi up but, for the time being, I was content to cruise. I also knew I was fitter than him and my stamina was greater. It seemed to take forever and ever, but I was pulling back a half a second here and there. So when there was only fifty yards between us, I'd knew I'd got him. I wanted to do him on the last lap, but three laps from the end as I was about to dive in, he looked down as if there was oil on his tyre.

I looked but couldn't see anything and so I gave him the thumbs-up sign and I went. It turned out it was his swinging arm that had gone, yet he said afterwards he hadn't felt anything until he accelerated into the next corner after I had overtaken him.

All I had to do was finish the race. Two laps, one lap, not very far now, I thought. Everyone had their thumbs up in the pits as I went past but there was still time to break down.

I was almost panicking, something was bound to go wrong. But as I reached the second from last right-hander, I knew there wasn't far to ride. At the last bend, I knew I could push it home from there, although I had made a rule I would never push a bike for very far because of my dodgy legs. It was flat and only 200 yards, and with almost a minute in hand on the second man, I felt I could make it.

But nothing did go wrong. Fifty yards from the flag, I finally realised I had done it. I thought: 'Out of sight.' I stood up on the foot-rests as I went under the flag. I had done it. I had bloody well done it! A wheelie across the line would have been appropriate but there was no rise to get the front up and, besides, I didn't want to snap the chain. I could have come off and hurt myself with only yards to go!

Was I chuffed? After I dismounted people seemed to be everywhere about me offering congratulations. The moment was fantastic. I had always thought the time when I had won my Grand Prix in Belgium in '71 was the finest hour but the feeling of elation on this particular day was just unbelievable.

The three most talked about riders in Europe — Agostini (1), Sheene and Read.

Frank, Don and Stephanie were the first to welcome me home but before the celebrations could begin I had to drink a big bottle of water to quench my thirst and then collect another set of laurels on the victory rostrum.

But to be quite honest, it wasn't the greatest moment of my life. It didn't exactly seem like that at the time. I suppose that was because all the spadework had been done before in previous rounds and I merely had to go through the formality of sewing the series up.

Later that evening, the true meaning of my accomplishment began to become apparent. I was world champion and the impact of the importance and prestige of the title was beginning to be driven home. It was a good feeling. No-one could take it away from me. No-one could say I hadn't earned it.

That night we drank our way through thirty bottles of champagne — and at Swedish prices of £14 a bottle. It was really super. A perfect night. Nearly all the Continental riders came up to offer their congratulations.

There were some that didn't bother at the prize-giving. They were mostly British riders who still feel their pride is hurt if a compatriot gets the major award. Some of the British are funny about moments such as that.

Blokes like Christian Estrosi, Dieter Braun and Lucchinelli were truly pumped at the awards ceremony that I had won the championship. I spotted little Angel Nieto, my friend from '71, and handed him a bottle of champagne. He had enjoyed a successful day too and he gave me a bottle of champers in return later that evening. But I can say that the only British racer, apart from Chas Mortimer, to slap me on the back and remark: 'Great, I'm pleased you won it,' was John Newbold or 'Joe Ninety' as we call him in the Suzuki camp. Jack Findlay said something that was really terrific: 'I'm glad you got it, son. You missed out on the Formula 750 championship last year and gave that to me. Now you've got your reward,' he said.

173

But what Jack didn't perhaps remember was that he gave the 750cc championship to me in '73 when he fell off in Hockenheim and handed it to me on a plate. So his winning the title last year was only fair.

When I surfaced some time the next day, the feeling of joy was still with me. I knew I wouldn't have to go to Finland to race for buttons, nor would I have to travel to Czechoslovakia, a country and a way of life I hate because I believe in freedom of speech and freedom of movement. I also believe in free enterprise, that's why I vote Conservative. But that's a different matter.

I cruised back to the ferry port at Gothenburg and just wanted to get home and relax. What was meant to be a complete rest though, turned out to be one of the busiest periods of my career with a constant stream of people coming over to Wisbech to talk to me. Still I didn't mind. I had something to really talk about.

If the bike had been behaving properly, I reckon we could have had the Formula 750 championship in '76 as well. In almost every round, I was well up. But the machine let me down badly. They were mechanical problems, not a mental attitude of my own part to save myself for the 500cc races.

There was no question of saving my best efforts for the smaller class. In Daytona, the opening round, the chain broke; in Venezuela the con-rod went; in Imola it was the oil seal; the water pump broke in Nivelles in Belgium; the gearbox gave up in Nogaro, in France, and the crank bust in the British round at Silverstone in the second leg. How's that for reliability!

But there was just as much time devoted to my 750-3's as was spent getting the 500's ready for action. The 'three' proved unreliable because it was being pushed so hard, well beyond its limit. I couldn't stay with 750cc Yamahas on the straights so it meant trying so damn hard on the corners that the bike was being overworked with all the

174

The final flourish. Barry Sheene prepares to take Tepi
Lansivuori in the Swedish Grand Prix and so become world
champion in the 500cc class

demands of being powered in and out of bends. It couldn't
stand the punishment.

But I was still giving a good show before it would give
up. I was pushing for second in Daytona when the chain
flew off, even though my Suzuki was way down on speed
compared to many other Yamahas. Venezuela was easier
because there were few big straights on such a short circuit.
I was catching Johnny Cecotto who was leading so, for
sure, the lowest I would have finished there would have
been second. I should have had a second at Imola if the oil
seal had not gone and I was leading both races at Nivelles
and at Nogaro. If it had been more reliable, no-one was to
say we couldn't have collected that award as well.

But my heart was obviously set on winning the 500cc
title. It was and always will be the top prize. The 500 was
more important and, besides, I had won the Formula 750
championship before.

In 1975 I finished in three rounds of the 750 competitions and won all three, so I had done my bit in that class. I did prefer to race the 750-3 when it was competitive but, in '76, it was so way behind on power compared with the Yamaha that it was no fun to ride. You knew you were as good as the other bloke who won but you were getting blown off on the Suzuki.

Naturally I must rate '76 as being the best year for me. Everything went right. But I can't complain about my luck. Ever since 1973, life's been good to me. The '73 season was a successful one, so was '74. I had my ups and downs in '75 but that was still good. I've had my fair share of the glory.

Yet I can still honestly say that I have only been out-ridden once, by Barry Ditchburn on his Kawasaki in the 1975 Post-TT meeting at Mallory. That day he beat me fair and square and there were no real excuses on my part. Since then no-one has out-ridden me.

The Canadian Steve Baker may have beaten me several times in '76 but it couldn't be said he out-rode me. His Yamaha was just far superior to anything my Suzuki could offer.

His Yamaha was a very fast motorbike. The only circuit where power doesn't matter is Mallory and I beat him there in the '76 Easter meetings. I had a tyre problem in the 'Race of the Year' later in '76 and so I couldn't get near the bloke. At Silverstone where it's all speed, he cake-walked the first leg of the John Player Grand Prix in '76 because of the fantastic power of his bike. Sure Steve's a good rider but I wouldn't say he was better than six other riders I could think of.

When I have been struggling to keep up, I have to rely on heavy braking and slow corners. I'm quicker than most on fast corners, certainly as quick as the best, but on slow bends when hard braking is required, I'm in my element. The chances of hurting yourself from falling off when braking hard are pretty slim. Often I have had the back wheel off the ground in those situations and once, at the Mallory hairpin while I was chasing Baker, I stood the bike on its nose and the tail must have been two feet in the air. I had messed up the start and seemed to be fighting a losing battle trying to catch Baker up. I was closing on him by a about a fifth of a second a lap but it just wasn't enough.

Of course, those match races that year caused me to be involved in one of my hairiest moments and, although it's a rare thing for me to admit, it has to be said that there was only me to blame. I was already top points scorer for Britain in the three-match series and I was keen to get a good placing to help our country in the final leg at Oulton.

The Gods were with me that day. Boy, was I lucky? I was too intent on watching Ron Haslam doing freaky things with his Yamaha in front of me. Because I didn't want him to centre-punch me, I had let him pass in the interests of personal safety. I came out of Fosters Corner and was convinced he was going to fall off. He couldn't swing the machine about like that and hope to stay on. So I was ready to avoid the bits and pieces. I grabbed a big handful of throttle and the bike just turned round sideways in the middle of the road. The tyre may have had something to do with it but it must be put down as my mistake. The bike was still going along as I was thrown up in the air. Fortunately I landed back on the bike, I snatched at the handbars but both my legs were on one side of the machine dragging on the tarmac. I smashed the screen and the rev counter but somehow managed to get the whole lot under control from 100 mph. Stupid of me to be so eaten up with what Ron Haslam was doing that I lost all my concentration. It taught me a lesson.

Going too fast or acts of misjudgement will very rarely lead me into a crash. I know the limitations of men and machines and so I act accordingly. But the Oulton near-disaster was definitely a blot on my copybook.

After I had clinched the world championship, the lure of travelling abroad any more that year diminished. I could have made a small fortune from appearing in major Continental meetings in the latter half of the year. An example was a meeting in Italy. The organisers offered me £8,000 to just have one 500cc ride. That was one of the biggest deals I could have been involved in.

But I was tired of rushing around the place all the time. It could be good fun seeing different people, eating local food and calling on loads of friends, but after a while it gets a bit wearing. My Rolls was new at the beginning of May that year. Yet three months later there were 13,000 miles on the clock.

So I rejected the Italian bid and settled to ride at the Hutchinson 100 meeting on the same day for less than half that offer. But money isn't everything. I wanted my first ride as world champion to be in front of my own fans and I have always liked the Hutch and the Brands circuit. My reward was to win all my three races at the meeting. Another reason to stay in Britain was to try to get that Superbike Championship title back from Kawasaki. It was an important award for both me and for Suzuki.

The American races don't have quite the same appeal for me now. The cost of just getting out there for rider, bikes and mechanics is enormous and the Stateside organisers don't pay start money or expenses. What a rip-off. The prize money might be attractive but the financial proposition as a whole isn't particularly appealing.

Judged on the way I feel about what I should or should not do, I suppose in nine cases out of ten I could be labelled the complete professional. Primarily I treat motorcycle racing as my sport but, in the same way, I try to work on a professional basis. If I really want to do something, I'll do it for nothing.

On the other hand, if I feel an organiser is trying to take me for a ride then they'll get no joy out of me. English promoters are good to deal with. They know me well enough. It's on the Continent that you have to be on the ball to watch out for unscrupulous organisers who will be out to fiddle you in some way.

That's why I'm always so careful to read the small print on any contract. It's about the only thing I do read apart from the motorcycling publications. I've never been a great lover of reading; it never interested me. I might flick through some of the 'horny' magazines like Playboy or Knave but that's about the extent of my literary interest.

The basic Suzuki contract fee, which Suzuki GB were having to find on their own after Suzuki Japan and Suzuki America quit racing as part of their world-wide cut-back programme, was largely the same as I received in 1975. Fortunately, Heron Suzuki had a major sponsor in Texaco, and Forward Trust, to a lesser degree, to help them out this time. Mashe may have been splashed all over the bike and my leathers that season but that was nothing to do with Suzuki. That was a private contract of my own with the French jeans company for whom I had to promise to wear their products when in the public eye. I always did as well!

Although I did not receive a rise in rates from Suzuki, I think the deal was fair. My record at the end of '75 showed I had not won one major honour which wasn't particularly brilliant for the Suzuki marketing image. And they were also handing over a lot of money at the beginning of 1976 to someone who looked to be having difficulty in merely getting out of bed let alone piloting a potential world-beating bike.

No, the offer made by Suzuki was satisfactory to me, certainly I had no complaints! Gross earnings for my work should have gone over £100,000 for the year. That's common knowledge now. But what people might not appreciate is that that hundred grand is a gross figure and by the time I have paid for all the nerks who work in the

179

income tax offices and and filled the pockets of those in the unemployment queues, I'm not left with so much bearing in mind that my money is taxed at something like eighty-odd pence in the pound.

I pay my dues just like most other respectable people but the taxation levels really seems to make nonsense of all the time, effort, not to mention danger, spent in becoming a top-line racer. There was talk of me emigrating at one stage to dodge the hefty taxes, but the thought of living abroad and not being able to race at home very much made it a fairly dismal idea.

My pay-outs should obviously improve in future seasons. Then I can call the tune with the world title behind me. But there'll be no screwing of organisers and promoters. That's not my style and never will be. I shall ask what I am worth. But it doesn't mean to say I will not go along with the boys when it comes to getting improved conditions in the way of safety standards and start money fees.

Ex-world champion Phil Read checks what the new world champion is up to at the start of the first leg of the 1976 British Grand Prix at Silverstone.

That cannot be an accusation levelled at me. The 'I'm all right Jack' saying just doesn't apply. In fact, I'm happy to lead any deputation or protest and it helps the cause being one of the more successful riders. The Belgium Grand Prix in 1976 was a good example of sensible race organisers understanding certain problems when they come from someone who believes he knows what he is talking about.

I asked for the race to be cut down by a couple of laps because the highly-developed tyres would not last the full distance at average speeds of over 125 mph for over 100 miles in temperatures that were well into the eighties. They understood and the race was reduced from twelve to ten laps.

But, taking all organisers into consideration, I should say that my relationship with them has always been good. We understand each other and we realise what a meeting is worth financially.

But although the Grand Prix organisers have their hands tied, they don't struggle much to change the set-up. The FIM have a laid-down scale of minimum start money fees paid on the basis of finishing in the table for that class the year before. I was sixth finisher in 1975 so I was number six on the pay scale. These are the bottom rates payable and the GP organisers often tend to go no higher. It seems an unreasonable way or sorting out the financial stakes and it did nothing for my bank balance.

International, non-championship meetings held in Europe, have always been the plum events for me. There the losses at GP's can be handsomely wiped out. Around £5,000 a time would be my 1977 average fee for that kind of race meeting. Perhaps it might be more or less depending on lots of different circumstances like my expenses to travel there, the state of the rate of currency exchange, the size of the anticipated crowd and the present feeling of demand for my appearance in that country.

As I have said, the world championships are a financial

disaster for me. Someone's making a lot of money out of them and it's definitely not the riders.

Look, I made a loss of around £200 on each Grand Prix I contested in 1976. To be fresh and in the right frame of mind, you have to stop in a decent hotel for a few nights for the meeting and in between while travelling there. If you can't stop somewhere where you can have a bath or shower, have a swim or a drink, I think your racing suffers. It's not a case of going overboard and spending like a madman; it's just day-to-day expense and in these days it gets worse every month.

By the time all my transport, ferry, petrol and meal costs are added up, every 1976 Grand Prix cost me about £500. Take away the average £300 start money payment and you can see each balance sheet does not look very healthy.

So although the world title was won, it wasn't worth a toss in terms of cash, although the sheer satisfaction of achieving it was reward enough. Pride is a pleasant enough sensation but it won't buy a new house or pay for the drinks cabinet to be filled up. So it was reassuring to think that the championship would increase my financial standing in the international meeting organisers' eyes.

Naturally, there are spin-offs and, coupled with the gradual upturn in the public acceptability of motorcycle racing, I began to receive a number of merchandising offers from various concerns to become involved with their products.

Time, as well as injuries, had restricted my activities in non-racing sidelines which could earn me a little bit of revenue in the years up to 1976, although I had been involved in various modelling assignments for magazines and newspapers. There was also the odd public appearance here and there but knowing how important 1976 would be to me, I had deliberately asked my agents who attract the attentions of the big businesses to play it down until the title was in the bag.

182

But, by then, Fabergé had me involved in making television commercials for Brut, the famous men's perfumery. They were featuring celebrities from all different sports and I was following after really famous names like Henry Cooper and David Hemery. After I had signed the contract to appear with our 'Enery, I remember I had dinner with Cary Grant, the film-star, who is connected with Fabergé.

Perfume is a matter of personal choice. My favourite smell is that of expensive scent for girls. I don't wear it myself, you must understand, only when I've been cuddling young ladies.

There are other advertising contracts in the pipeline and now a firm are likely to produce small models of me and my machine similar in size and design to those in the 'Action Man' series.

I've been fortunate to have one major network TV film on me and there's another one due to be screened in 1977.

Not only did the Brut advertising help me to become better known, it should have done much for motorcycle racing through the identification of the sport in the TV commercials. Some people still don't appreciate how big our sport now is.

Coverage of bike racing has never been good on both TV and in non-specialist publications but it's slowly getting better and it is something all of us connected with it must work hard at. For instance, every year all the motorcycling newspapers and magazines should get together to nominate one rider for fans to vote for in the major television and national paper 'sportsman of the year' polls. It's not necessarily me I'm thinking of. Let's just have one rider put forward annually who can win for the image of motorcycle sport.

That's entirely in the hands of spectators and, heavens above, there are enough of them for our sport to succeed. Personally I find fans at race meetings present more and more of a problem with each meeting. Perhaps it's not quite fair to describe them as a problem because if they weren't there, I perhaps wouldn't be paying surtax. Abroad it's easier because there is more time to sign autographs and talk to keen spectators especially with the Grands Prix spread over three days including practice.

But in England, with all the action packed into a solitary day and with four bikes to look after, it can be difficult to appear constantly approachable and friendly. My policy in '76 was to leave a spare hour free after the racing just for signing purposes. That's the best moment to catch me.

But the following was truly enormous in 1976 and there were some incredible sights as young people jostled and pushed for my signature. At Cadwell, two girls had a stand-up fight outside my parents' caravan in a race to get my autograph and Frank waded in to split them up. Another time a teenage girl was wielding a pair of scissors and she wanted to snip off a lock of my hair as a memento. After the Transatlantic Trophy series at Oulton I had to be smuggled out through the back window of the caravan in order to escape the pack. All good fun!

My incoming mail is often fairly heavy with fan mail. In the height of the season I must receive around 150 letters a week just from people with an interest in my fortunes. It gets impossible to answer all of them like I did a few years ago although my secretary deals with many.

Soon after winning the world title, I received a little note from the headmaster of my junior school which I thought was fantastic of him to remember me after all those years. Incredible of him to want to remember me because I was a horror to him. The letter was addressed to: 'Barry Sheene, Motorcycle Racer, Wisbech' and it said: 'Congratulations — but do please be careful.' I appreciated that note. On the subject of mail, another letter came from a fan in Spain addressed: 'Barry Sheene, Costa del Wisbech, GB'. It found me all right!

What A Life

In my well-thumbed passport are the stamps of dozens of foreign customs posts. If I travel by air, my arrival at these points of entry is never anything more than a routine checkout by the uniformed blokes. I am just another face in the crowd.

But when I go to a European meeting in my navy blue Rolls Royce, I know I can sometimes expect to get a royal welcome by the men manning the barriers. Naturally I have to go through the same customs routine as any other traveller from one country to another but as soon as they spot the '4 BS R' number plate and notice the occupation in my passport as 'Motorcycle Racer', some of them greet me like a long-lost brother.

A few of the Italian customs officials have made me smile on occasions because they're so demonstrative. Once I was coming down through the Dolomite mountains across from Switzerland and the jovial Italian frontiersman grasped my passport, threw back his happy face and boomed: 'Mister Sheene — You beat Agostini, yes?' I replied: 'I'll have a good go — but I hope you let me out if I do!'

But later at my hotel I reflected on the incident and thought about the significance of that simple early morning conversation. I must be famous I thought, if a person living in a tiny primitive village miles from any big town knew me and my profession.

Mind you, Italians have a passion for motorcycle racing that few nations can match, and their delight in seeing their favourite rider win a big event is something bordering on the unbelievable. It must be their hot Latin blood but I

185

have never seen such excitement from spectators anywhere else in the world when they have the opportunity to salute a winner. Agostini is usually their man, or was, until he hurt Italian pride by switching from the homeland concern of MV to Yamaha after the 1974 season.

Piggy in the middle.

The adulation and hero-worshipping of the fans is quite astonishing in countries with warmer climates than ours. They love to hoist you shoulder high and parade you around the track. I must admit I love all that and am happy to be involved in such scenes. But that sort of thing would never happen in Britain. Can you imagine Silverstone race-goers tossing me skywards around about Woodcote Corner? If it happened I bet the Auto Cycle Union would draw up a clause in their regulations forbidding it.

Yet I have to be careful how much rough treatment my body gets now. The Daytona and Mallory accidents in 1975 left me pretty fragile around the legs which I have to treat with great respect. Together they have stopped me bending my knees when I want to adopt a kneeling position. If I want to get down, I have to bend from the waist now. Often when I'm sitting down in the paddock at a race meeting, someone might come along and innocently give my leg a playful squeeze while chatting to me. Boy, that hurts and I have to tell people it does.

But for all the pain and the back-slapping, I am just an ordinary guy who makes his living out of riding a motorcycle in front of folks prepared to pay for the privilege of watching.

All right, I have had things going for me over the past few years — forgetting the prangs — and now I am about the best-known racer in Europe and perhaps am regarded as the top British rider by enthusiasts in America and Austrialia. That little moment with the Italian customs official was the earliest realisation that I was becoming something of a personality, but it took a world championship title in 1976 to bring it home to everyone who was into racing that I was the top dog.

So I am the best in Europe at road racing and what does it mean? It has helped to swell my bank balance for sure and I hope to reap further benefits in the coming seasons. But taking into account the publicity afforded to sport in general, I must be a complete unknown to thousands of people who reckon to have a working knowledge of sporting pursuits.

I am a British world champion of a sport that is the most dangerous and, arguably, the most demanding of any, yet the column inches in the national press devoted to the feats of my professional colleagues and I borders on the pathetic sometimes. Legions follow motorcycle racing in Britain every week and proof of the spectacular upsurge in interest is the record-breaking crowds at tracks, big and small, all over the country in 1976.

It's a sport in which Britain has a fair chance of going to the Continent and coming back with the heads of its sportsmen held high instead of returning saying they 'finished an honourable fourth in the face of extremely stiff opposition' and all that balls. It's strange how this country can breed good word-class motorcycle racers. It has a fine history of turning out riders who can make strong men gasp at the twitch of a throttle.

But for all the accolades the daily papers have given us, you would think the sport did not exist. Take the Transatlantic Trophy match races between Britain and America at Easter in 1976 for example. It's a super event and the wizard who dreamt up the idea should be knighted. The racing is always good and the riders on view are about the best in the world. No wonder knowledgeable race fans flock to the circuits wherever they appear.

The first meeting at Brands Hatch on the Good Friday of 1976 must have attracted around 40,000 people, the thought of which might just have brought a suspicion of a smile to the face of race promoter Chris Lowe. He is the kind of chap who doesn't delight in the massed banks of spectators just relieved of a few quid. Instead he hunts around the circuit looking for tell-tale gaps in the sea of faces and seems to appear worried if he discovers a square foot of grass not covered by a paying customer. But Chris knows his job inside out and he will share with me the incredible reaction of the National Press to that terrific day's racing.

I could only manage a second and a third in the two legs of the Trophy series and our visitors from across the Atlantic wowed everyone with their performance, with their star rider Steve Baker smashing the lap record for the Kent track.

It was reckoned thousands of motorists were held up in jams on the Swanley by-pass and all roads leading to the circuit, so there were many who missed the racing, and because of the location of Brands a whole host of racing fans would not have made the trip because of the distance involved.

So when I picked up my daily paper the next morning I was keen to see how much coverage it was given. I looked through the sports pages one way, then again and when I scratched through for a third time and realised there was nothing, I was amazed. Yet in my paper there was a prominent space devoted to an obscure show-jumping event at Hickstead, made memorable, it seemed, because a horse bolted from the ring and killed a dog.

Yet this was a typical example of the people in charge of the sports pages not knowing anything, or not wanting to know anything, about bike racing. How many times have you seen considerable column inches in the morning papers given over to minority sports such as bowls, swimming or sailing. OK, so quite a lot of people take an active part in these pastimes but in no way do they compare with the numbers that watch or are involved in motorcycle racing.

I maintain that bikes are more dangerous to race than cars and require more skills to compete on them at the speeds they are capable of. But just look at the publicity the car boys get. James Hunt, although he's a friend of mine and a great driver in my opinion, has only to sneeze and he has a gallery of pressmen around him.

The problem of motorcycle racing taking a down-the-chart rating can safely be said to be due to a couple of reasons. The sport still retains a grubby image in some quarters you know, dirty leather jackets, long hair and hell-raisers on noisy bikes. The bad happenings by yobbos at the British GP's at Silverstone haven't helped either. This opinion is a common one shared by the people who have only heard of Geoff Duke and still regard motorcycles as for those who cannot afford cars as a means of transport.

It's going to take a lot of educating to prove to all of them that bike racing is now glamorous and motorbikes have never been more acceptable. My efforts have helped to get the sport extra publicity, I'm sure, and the situation can only improve.

This inferior attitude to the two-wheelers of the track has not been helped by many sports editors of the national papers who get nought out of ten for observation. They have stuck to the traditional sports of soccer, horse racing and cricket to try to keep their circulation ticking over and to have one of those persons attend a major motorcycle race meeting in this country would be something of a sensation.

They must be aware of its existence but cannot be bothered to see for themselves how strong the cause is. A journey out of Fleet Street to the Race of the Year or the British Grand Prix would convince them that here is a sport with a following as good as any other and one which contains a rich vein of home-spun talent. If they included motorcycle racing in the Olympic Games, Britain would scoop gold, I can tell you.

But to be fair to those lads who do their bit for us racers, I should say there are one or two columnists who do their best to squeeze in as much as they can into a confined space. George Turnbull of the Daily Telegraph and Leslie Nicholl of the Daily Express are two of them. In fact,

George is quite a character in his own way. Always a man with a keenness for alcohol, I wondered why he had been delayed in getting to the hotel bar after one particular Grand Prix. 'I was washing my smalls and my shirts, dear chap,' he replied. 'But I discovered you can only get one shirt at a time in the lavatory pan.' I am still not sure to this day whether he was joking or not!

So I am king of my profession, though still largely unknown to the masses. But I shall not lose too much sleep over that. Unfortunately the only time I made the front pages of the national dailies was when the news leaked out about my friendship with Stephanie McLean. I suppose that sort of thing occurs every day of the year but as I am in the public eye — even in a small way — and it tied up nicely with James and Suzy Hunt's marriage break-up, I made the headlines. It's a pity they couldn't have feted me as the man who thrashed Agostini and company at 150 mph.

My friendship with Stephanie blossomed from the winter of late '75 and she seemed to bring me luck through the world championship campaign. We were both born under the same sign of the Zodiac, Virgo, if that means anything, but we found we had so much in common, both in our interests, our attitudes to life and with our personalities.

There have been few occasions when we argued and it was so peaceful and pleasant knowing that she was around all the time. As people who have followed my career will know, I have always been noted as having more than a passing interest in females. As the fame increased and the Sheene image seemed to grow larger with each day, I was being allowed the opportunities that all young, healthy men often crave for.

Wherever I went, I would have no trouble finding a girl. And travelling around made it easier to meet so many lovely young ladies. But it seemed to get into a routine every time I went off to a Grand Prix or international. Instead of giving complete dedication and concentration all of the time to my machines and the task that lay ahead, I would have to spend some time exploring the locality for a bird. There was no shirking of my racing responsibilities in any way. I certainly endeavoured to perform to the best of my ability . . . both on and off the track.

But when I had Stephanie by me, I was really contented. It doesn't sound like Sheene talking but it was true to say I'd found the woman who made my life happy. There seemed to be even more available birds around in '75 but they just didn't interest me at all. And it looked as if Stephanie was my good luck charm.

As far as my personality goes it's best left to others to judge whether there has been a marked change in me since success started happening to me in a big way. I think I am no different from when I first started to race the Bultaco in the late Sixties. I still like to be pleasant to people, I have retained my sense of humour, although maybe it's a bit more sophisticated now, and I like to get maximum enjoyment out of life as I did when roughing it around Europe as a budding racing mechanic.

Naturally my circumstances and situation have changed. I have worked for my wealth. But just because I have a Rolls Royce, a few investments, a home in the country and another in London and generally live well, I am still the kind of happy-go-lucky guy you might see in any street on his way to meet a girl or going off to the pub. Except that I don't meet other girls now 'out of working hours' and neither do I often go to pubs. The girl situation I have just explained and I don't often have the time or inclination to sit boozing in pubs either. If you took me into a pub and gave me a pint of bitter, I couldn't drink it. Possibly it's the way I'm made but I am unable to down beer in quantities amounting to more than half a pint. It just blows me out and, yes, I am conscious of the fact that beer can make you fat. I don't think I have ever seen a fat racer so I wouldn't like to be the first.

By saying I'm not an aleman might knock my popularity with the heavy bike brigade, but although I never drink to excess, I do like either a glass of good wine, brandy and ginger, or an occasional vodka and tonic when I am relaxing with company. During a race meeting I always stick to soft drinks, or mineral water if abroad. If I drink in moderation, the same cannot be said for my smoking habits.

It would be useless to count how many I puff away each day, but a daily dose of forty-five would be a conservative estimate, and that's a cut-back on a few years ago! My preference is for strong untipped cigarettes such as Gauloises but I'll smoke whatever is being handed around. There's one journalist I know who always has to buy a fresh pack of twenty every time he comes to see me because I never seem to have any at the time and scrounger Sheene will get through them in an hour while information for the article is being collated. I hope his boss believes him when he submits his expenses claim.

Eating quality food is another aspect of my changing lifestyle. Whereas before I would be happy as an underpaid, undernourished, scraggy mechanic to stuff myself with sausages or beans, I have learned to appreciate the culinary delights of first class cooking. It's still grub, I know, but I am keen on items on a quality restaurant menu that are fairly exotic by normal standards.

Apart from eating well and doing happy things with my girlfriend, I don't suppose I have much in the way of hobbies. Dining is a serious preoccupation with me. Most food that is non-greasy and well-prepared goes down well. But even though I might be the original Cockney kid, fish and chips is out. Hate that kind of stuff. But basic fare like beans on toast is fine. I use to get through plenty of beans when I first roughed it around Europe. It's just horrible, fatty food I can't stand.

I'm quite partial to genuine authentic foreign food but not the rubbish the Chinese and Indian places over here serve up. If there is one favourite dish, I suppose it has to be steak cooked delicately in a pleasant wine sauce washed down with a gentle white wine. I'm just as happy with well-cooked game or fish. If I'm at home and either Steph or mother is doing the meal, then I will tuck into spaghetti bolognese as happily as anyone.

Dinner is usually my main meal of the day. Or tea as I still call it. I often get up late in the morning and if it's not a bowl of Sugar Puffs, I frequently feel like eggs in some form for breakfast — scrambled on toast, boiled, poached, perhaps fried sometimes. Two cups of 'Rosy Lee' and a few cigarettes will set me up for the rest of the day, although I might just have a salad in summer or a sandwich during the cooler months at lunchtime. I have never been a big eater, as my build might suggest.

In fact, someone once said I had the waist of a woman. I'm not sure what he meant by that but I'm only twenty-eight inches around the waist, my shorts and jeans are also worn by Stephanie who, like me, also has long legs. Being overweight has never been a problem as I've always kept to around just under ten stones. My bad days as a sick school-boy probably account for me not being built like a bull.

But my sport calls for a lot of physical effort and being a motorcycle racer does require a high level of fitness especially as the Formula 750 races last 200 miles. That's a long time to ride a bike almost to the limit during what are usually the hottest months of the year.

Knowing that some of these races can be human endurance races when the going gets tough on the shorter twisty circuits, I pushed myself harder than ever before at the end of 1975 to get into an ideal physical shape. To most people on the outside I appeared a crock. If I'd have been a footballer I'd have been advised to hang up my boots. And if I was a racehorse, I'm sure I would have been shot. That's what so many were thinking at the time.

Realising that it was going to take more than nature's normal healing powers of time to be in tip-top shape for the new campaign in 1976, I got down to business in a big way.

Press-ups began to become a part of my early-morning life as I pushed my body up and down, up and down, as many times as my arms could stand. Waist bends, shoulder exercises, in fact any aspect of torso movement figured prominently in my programme.

Despite the eighteen-inch steel pin neatly aligned in my left thigh, almost down to my knee, I tried my damnest to get those legs of mine back to some semblance of the condition that had been adequate for the previous twenty-four years.

I had never been a super-athletic feller at the best of times, but this was for real. My whole career rested upon being truly fit. So I swam and I hobbled, as best I could. When I had discarded first one walking stick and then, thankfully, the other, I knew I was on the way.

My movements were slow and laboured and getting from one point to another seemed to take an eternity. Knee bends were out of the question but I was just happy to have mobility to transport my body whenever I decided to make a move.

The left leg was not really the trouble. The Daytona crash had messed it about in a complicated way. If it had been a clean break of the bone, a couple of months would have put me right. But coming off at 175 mph meant it was a completely different set of circumstances and so it was only to be expected to have something of a different injury with the poor old peg compressed in the crash.

It was the right leg that caused me the anxiety over

whether or not I would be able to make the season in time. The thought of being ready for the first big meeting at Daytona in March 1976 seemed to numb the pain. Believe me, I was suffering with that broken knee. The pain-killing injections stopped the throbbing agony for a brief interval but relief would only be short-lived.

Modern medical science in the form of the University College Hospital in London, just a short walk from where I first learned to ride a motorcycle, worked wonders for me. Needless to say I was walking as normally as the next man by early spring and without a trace of a limp or a mince or anything that would suggest that six months before I found it hell just coming down the stairs for my breakfast.

The body is an incredible thing really. One minute I was clattering helplessly about on crutches, then next I was well enough to get on the dance floor for a short burst although most of the movement was a sort of gyroscopic effect from the torso. Yet most of the time I had no difficulty driving the Rolls, mainly because hardly any knee movement was required in an automatic car.

One of the other important thing that aided my swift recovery was living in a Chelsea town-house owned by Piers Forester. It was just a big goal kick away from the Chelsea football ground and had enough room to get the Rolls in the driveway without the tail sticking too much into the road.

To say Piers is crazy would be unfair. But some of the things he has done makes my life as an international racer seem as mundane as the nine-to-five vocation of a White-hall civil servant.

Piers is an Old Harrovian, comes from a titled Irish family with a castle back home in Ireland and has a splendid way with words. He has run a trucking company, has been employed to recover bikes where the hire purchase payments have not been kept up and must have done lots

196

of other jobs before I knew him. When I lived with him and his Australian mechanic, John, he'd be away for days on end on some particular kind of work all in the cause of helping to finance his racing.

Yes, he's the man who for twelve months took out Princess Anne before she married. Incredible, but it's true and knowing his zany behaviour, anything was possible with him. He once won a marathon motorcycle rally, the Raid Orion, from Paris to Turkey, and has been involved in several brushes with the law throughout the world, for nothing worse, I should add, than motoring offences. In Daytona in 1975, he had to be bailed out in time for practice after doing 70 mph along the front where there was a 10 mph speed limit.

One night when there was a Chelsea home match, Piers did something horrible to a bloke's windscreen because his car was parked in his drive and he couldn't get his own motor into the garage. Not long ago, Piers was arrested in Paris for being involved in some mix-up over an unpaid petrol bill.

But his brand of way-out humour went down well with me and with a constant stream of racing friends and lovely young ladies around the place most days, it was a really happy, open house.

The atmosphere must have helped my general disposition because I know if I had been holed up on my own during the weeks of recuperation I would have brooded over my injuries.

Provided no social engagements — and there were many — interfered with my programme, I would nearly always go back to my home at Walton Highway at the weekend, usually in the company of a female companion.

Pheasant shooting I found quite relaxing. I'm not a dead-shot but I maintain a steady trigger hand. With friends from London, we would visit the Fens on winter shooting trips and that's how I first spotted my house. It was completely derelict at the time, almost falling down. Everywhere was overgrown with hedges and weeds and the grass was four feet high. There was an old abandoned lorry chassis in one corner of the grounds and generally the place was just a dump.

It took a lot of hard work and sweat to get the place round after I had decided I fancied the surroundings the house stood in. The place had to be fully modernised although with the help of friends and men in my race team like mechanic Don and driver John, we got the place habitable. Once I was merrily operating a tractor in the pouring rain moving some rubbish when suddenly the whole machine slid into an adjoining dyke with me aboard! But all the effort was worthwhile and now there's room to live and move about there.

The back roads around home are fairly quiet and they can make good test tracks when we've completed some

Mum and dad, Stephanie and Barry, look happy with life.

changes on the bikes. But the ripples in the lanes really provide some good wheelie action.

Usually riders, pressmen, photographers and even just autograph hunters are constantly popping in to see me and my six cats, creatures I'm very fond of because they're gentle and soft and can respond without a lot of coaxing.

I never shun anybody when I'm at home. Callers are welcome if they have come on a specific purpose. My phone number is not even ex-directory but sometimes I wish it was with the amount of calls that have to be answered.

But generally peace reigns there. In complete contrast to the noise and excitement of the race tracks, the only thing that can be heard at home is the wind through the poplar trees at the bottom of the paddock or the occasional Fen tractor chugging along the lane. The surrounding area is as flat as a pancake but the Fens have a certain charm for me.

Even though I've a four-bedroomed terraced house near the Thames at Putney in London, Walton Highway will continue to be my main home. It's just useful to have a base to operate from in London. I've never severed my connections with London and I want to retain my ties with the capital. Walton Highway is no picture postcard village; it has a couple of pubs, a garage, a shop, and a chippie and is centred on the main road to the North Norfolk coast. My house, Ashwood Hall, lies off the trunk route and needed a fair bit of attention before it could be described as comfortable.

It seemed right that my parents should live there after all they had done for me and, although the quiet and solitude of the locality took them by surprise initially, they have both settled down there well. Franco's happy because he can potter around in the workshops which are converted stables. There's often a couple of bikes there for him to tinker with if he isn't kept busy by people calling on him for mechanical advice.

My mother likes the countryside too. But she's been a super-mum to me, a real inspiration when my spirits were low, and I guess she could adapt to any change in her way of life. She sometimes goes off to Spain, with my sister Maggie and her nipper, where my parents have a villa on the Mediterranean coastline. She deserves holidays with the number of times she has to answer the phone when I'm away.

Back home I can unwind. I never encourage people to visit me at weekends because I value the privacy of my retreat and am grateful on occasions to get away from the hub-bub of racing. I can drift around the gardens, watch the box or get stuck into one of those excellent French motorcycle magazines. Do anything I want, when I want.

My six-bedroomed house stands in about four acres and is bordered by an apple orchard. With the grounds it's in, it should be worth £40,000 at current market prices.

The photographers and reporters know where I hang out now and, although they seem to come more often these days, I don't find their visits too much bother.

One gorgeous female photographer on an assignment for a specialist magazine began to lose some of her nervousness by the time she had a third glass of brandy; Sheene measures are never short! So she asked me to show her my bedroom, which is dominated by a big circular bed, and complemented with stereo, television and sun-ray light system. Well, that sort of invitation I am unable to turn down. But she wanted a picture taken in surroundings that mirrored my off-track character. Heaven knows why she should think of my bedroom.

Those people who have seen my bedroom reckon it's like a tailor's shop with rail upon rail of trousers and shirts. At the last count, I think I had twenty jackets, thirty pairs of trousers, sixty pairs of jeans and around a couple of hundred shirts. Casual clothes such as jeans and soft shirts make me feel far more comfortable. And stand up the man who last saw me wearing a tie, I only own three!

I'm fortunate to earn enough money to indulge in expensive French clothes, quite a lot of which come from a little mother-and-daughter shop tucked away in one of those many back-streets off Oxford Street in London. I reckon it's the cut of French clothes that make them appear so much classier. Italian wear is much the same. But extra quality always leads to a higher price. My shoes, too, are Continental, either made in Spain or Italy. I like them to be of real leather in a soft low-cut style.

If I say I like to dress in neat clothing, I know a score of folks who would laugh their socks off. Most of the time when I'm racing in the sunshine countries, I truck around the paddock in an ancient pair of sawn-off denim shorts and a battered pair of dusty sandals.

But even so, a few modelling jobs have come my way in the past, one of the first being for the posh Vogue magazine. Yet one picture that remains fairly clear in many people's memories shows me in just a pair of underpants. Perhaps they do just want me for my body! I enjoyed that kind of work because you were into a friendly set and there were chances of getting to know some of the leading models.

Why choose me to model clothes? Well, all right, I may not be Mr. Universe but my compact measurements and fairly long legs are apparently the ideal attributes for that line of work. Obviously, being something of a name in the motorcycling game helped matters and I am confident that, being world champion at last and leading a sport that must soon get big media coverage, many more modelling assignments will come my way.

But if I sound flash or something of a poseur, let me put the record straight. I now lead a pretty glamorous life and move in circles inhabited by influential people. So my lifestyle has changed from when I first started racing. But that does not mean I have changed.

The money may have improved the way I live but it has done little to alter my character. I'm still devoted to my parents; Christ, I still live with them — and I have not tuned off the same wavelength I was on a few years back in the days of lorry-driving, sleeping rough in the back of Ford Transit Vans and swearing like a trooper.

Forget the cash aspect. Just compare me with any other middle-class bloke in his mid-twenties. Most get enjoyment out of eating, drinking, sleeping, pulling birds, maybe watching a film or taking part in a sport. Well that's me too. Just because I push a couple of wheels around at fast speeds at Silverstone one week, the Salzburgring the next instead of pushing a pen behind a desk in Potter's Bar, it shouldn't set me apart from the rank and file of British bachelors.

Take pop music for instance. I'm as clued up on Barry White or Rod Stewart as the next man. I like modern music in almost any form and on the back seat of the Rolls for every trip is a big box of cassettes for the quadrophonic stereo.

Image building is now a vital ingredient of modern-day sporting success stories and I suppose I have done as much as anyone to promote my name, as well as for the cause of motorcycle racing. Everything seems to be on my side now and I want to make the most of a good situation.

But the popular opinion of a motorcycle racing champion is still not a good one. Well I may not speak as smoothly as Mike Hailwood or Phil Read did, but I think I am just as sharp as either of them.

It doesn't take me long to get my sums right and I know now precisely what to say, and when to say it when the occasion arises. I can speak Spanish fluently and am getting better all the while with French and Italian. And I didn't have to go to night school either.

So don't let anyone write me off as the poor man's champion. My knowledge of machinery is sound. My

A quiet chat with brother-in-law Paul Smart.

knowledge of men becomes greater with each day, and I can honestly say with no fear of contradiction, I have done more for the sport in the last three or four years than anyone else.

As far as Britain goes, I have revived a flagging interest. I know my presence can put another 10,000 on the gate at any track here. In France, Holland or Italy, you can double that figure. Cock to those who claim I'm too gay, too frivolous and too big-headed for the racing game. I'm taking motorcycles as fast as they have ever gone and every time on every track I'm out to win. If I succeed, then I've achieved my objective and I'm happy.

Mostly it makes the crowds happy too — and that's the way it should be. I know the Establishment in racing, the senior citizens who somehow are still involved in the running of bike races, will always regard me as a teenage tearaway because of my carefree approach to life and living. Well they're entitled to their opinions just as much as I am to mine . . . and I have never been slow to seize any opportunity to express my feelings when I reckon I've had a raw deal.

As a representative for the sport, my qualities are as good as most others and from my lofty perch of world champion I shall be hoping to make the riders' lot a much more rewarding one.

Often in interviews the questioning gets around to my personality, and the reporter frequently expresses surprise when I say there is hardly any aggressiveness in my character. Even if I break down in a race, I never ever feel the need to be bitter or angry. My family and friends are the best judge of me but I would always describe myself as being friendly and generally happy with life.

But I act the way I feel and if I don't feel pleasant towards someone it's pretty obvious what my feelings are. My emotions are never covered up.

Jealousy exists in most sports and motorcycle racing is

no exception, but I have always figured that instead of being envious of someone it is always better to go out to try to do something better yourself.

There's no point in being jealous. We are all born with the same amount of grey matter upstairs and if people don't make full use of it in the best possible way, it's their fault entirely that the breaks don't come. And if you do everything yourself there's only one person to blame when things go wrong — yourself.

There was a time when I didn't have money. I've worked bloody hard to get to the top but I haven't ridden rough-shod over many people to achieve that target. I reckon I've been a fair ambassador for the sport and if an interview or story is required, I'll do it, even if there might be some-thing controversial as the general theme. Why should I worry what people think about what I say? There will always be those who reckon you're saying the wrong things or doing something that is not quite right.

What I've mentioned about people's envy streak may be very apparent when considering all the publicity and glamour that surrounds my job. It's part and parcel of my profession and I have come to accept it as being just another piece of a professional sportsman's way of life. It does prove that I am earning my money from Suzuki and the different race promoters.

But I can honestly say that I have never put on a deliberate publicity stunt for the benefit of the press to further my own cause. Everything I have done in the past has merely been part of my normal life. There has never been any need for acts.

All the attention afforded me since success came my way will not affect me, I'm sure of that. Back in 1971 I did become a little callous about all the good things that were happening to me and maybe I was weakening. But I grew up and with good results over the last two or three years, I'm used to the pressures of success. I realised in '71 that all the fuss associated with winning could be my downfall and I reckoned I'm cured of being a bit of a big-head.

No matter how pressing needs may be or how vast the number of people chasing me is, if there is something I want to do on my own, I'll do it. I'm getting more settled in life now specially after meeting Stephanie. But talk of being tied down is rubbish. I'm in this position because I want to be. If I was being dictated to, and it applies to everything, I would soon rebel. Because what I like to do is acceptable to Stephanie, there are no restrictions placed on me.

But marriage won't lead to the quiet life for me. In fact, doing something less hectic than bike racing has never appealed to me. I've always to be my own boss because the thought of working for somebody turns my stomach over.

I was born to lead, I reckon, rather than to be led and that statement applies to more than just the races. It's my independent nature. Possibly that outlook puts more pressure on me to succeed and I know that, as world champion, the demand for me, my name and constant winning grows greater all the time. The times are becoming more frequent when the crowds warm to another rider who has a chance of beating me. That's life. I experienced it all before when the crowd were willing me as an underdog to beat Read or Ago.

Now it's Grant or Ditchburn or Haslam many folks seem to get behind if they think they will give me a hard time. It doesn't bother me, pressures like that never will. It's just part of the racing game.

Another aspect, as I have mentioned before, is the number of hangers-on it attracts. I know stacks and stacks of people through racing, but when the chips are down I have really only about five or six friends I can count on. That's just about the ideal situation for a person in my position and I'm happy about it.

Obviously the future and what is in store often crops up

Every picture tells a story. That's why all those photographs stuck on his office wall hold special memories for him.

in my thoughts. There are no plans laid as yet. I want to earn a lot more money out of racing and then when I give up the sport get down to sorting out a career for the rest of my life. finance is the important thing and, like everyone else, I have to safeguard my future.

As it is at the moment, I want to get enough out of racing so I don't have to work like a bastard when it's time to quit. But that won't happen at the very earliest until I'm at least thirty. Barring any accidents, I know I'll be around the top until then and maybe for a bit longer.

There will be people coming up, of course, but what class rider hasn't has to contend with that problem? Look at Read. There must have been dozens of promising names rising through the ranks during his career but he is still one of the top runners after twenty years.

A combination of different factors may have reduced the number of potential world champions but I'm not complaining. That must be good for me. But seeing one man dominate all the big races will not be too good for the sport, nor will it go down too well with the spectators. That argument was proved right when Ago dominated everything and people began to become a little disenchanted when there was no-one else to challenge him.

But what can I do? I realise that some do not like me to win all the time. But you race motorcycles for a factory or sponsor. They're interested in winning. I'm interested in winning. And the crowds are interested in you winning.

On the other hand, when you win too much, the crowd's interest wanes to a degree, but if you don't come in first in ten races they're mad for you to win again. But there's no way I am not going to win for ten races just to keep some people happy.

Anyway, I'll do my best to entertain and to carry on the way I have done on the tracks — riding hard and fast and fair in the manner that has pulled back the crowds in some small way and I won't disagree when they say I have put the fun back into road racing.

But when my racing comes to an end I would like to get into some kind of business. What that will be it is too early to say. Markets and trends can change so quickly. Look at the car trade. That looked a sure-fire winner not so long ago. Now it's not quite such a safe bet. You can never tell what will be a good thing to be in. It may not be something I have had an interest in before.

It'll be a business or enterprise that I will become involved in for one thing — to make money. I will not be doing it for the love of it. Just something I can earn a bloody good living out of, although naturally I will have some interest in the goings-on so that I can give my best. One thing is certain, my ties with sport will never be severed. I'll be connected in some way, maybe as a sponsor.

Negotiating the bale-lined corner, Sheene chases more spoils in an international in France.

Me & My Bikes

No matter how good a rider is, his chances of success hinge upon the quality and reliability of his machine. Even with one hundred per cent fitness, superb course knowledge and a rare brand of riding skill, you will be nowhere without the right raceware.

Looking back over the years, there have been some riders who have been better than their machines and, quite honestly, there have been bikes that were superior to their handlers.

Johnny Cecotto has proved that on a reliable motorcycle he is a match for nearly everyone; put him on inferior bikes like the junk he had in '76 and the boy is an also-ran. But I rate him as a terrific competitor and on the right mounts may prove to be unstoppable.

Agostini had the finest machines around during that lengthy spell in the late Sixties in the MV Agusta hey-days and he blew everyone off. But when Phil Read came along on the same bike and beat him, it seemed Ago was not the brilliant rider he was cracked up to be. He was lucky to have it easy for so long. I certainly will not be bothered how strong the opposition is over the next few years.

Having been with Suzuki since 1973, I have not experienced racing on too wide a range of machines, but what I have ridden have all been useful apart from the works Yamahas in '72. I had a disastrous time with them; it was one thing after another and after a while I began to think: 'Is it the bike that's going wrong? Or is it me?'

I had ridden Yamahas fairly successfully before but nothing went right when I had the golden opportunity to land works bikes. A world championship title was my aim after going so close in the 125cc class the year previously and I fancied my chances on the 250 water-cooled Yammy. That was I did until the Grands Prix got underway.

In the opening world championship round at the Nurburgring in West Germany the 250 seized on the fourth lap. When it came to a halt, I said to myself: 'Mmm, just one of those things.' A friendly German by the rallings helped to console me by giving me some steins of some marvellous local beer which I enjoyed although I am not a beer drinker.

I did manage to pick up eight points for fourth spot in the Austrian GP but I was beginning to worry about the situation. John Dodds beat me for third place, and he was only an ordinary air-cooled Yamaha TD2 which was already two years old.

Press on, I thought, because Yamaha are no mugs and this little twin-engined thing of mine must come good soon. New barrels were fitted to the bike before the Italian round and I felt pretty confident. But on the first practice session, on the first lap would you believe, a piston ring peg broke and the whole lot seized. I crashed to the ground, bust my left collar-bone badly and knocked myself unconscious. My stomach was also badly cut. What a mess. I was beginning to realise that I shouldn't have jumped so quickly at the chance to ride Yamaha.

That Italian job was about the worst blow of all and even though I managed some reasonable results in international meetings later that year, it was obvious to me the 250cc Yamaha was no world championship contender in its present form.

It was a bad year for me, a bad year for that blessed little two-stroke. My rating must have tumbled in Yamaha's eyes because I had achieved nothing to enhance their reputation. I hadn't done my career much good either.

The Yamaha works technicians rarely paid any attention to suggestions I made that might have helped make the bike more reliable and faster. They appeared suspicious of me, imagining that I was some young long-haired second-rater who had so much to prove on the race tracks. It was all so annoying. The bloody bike was slower than the air-cooled machines produced the year before and it was obvious to all that something drastic needed to be done to make it competitive. Rod Gould was my partner on the other works water-cooled 250. He had proved himself a highly-capable rider by winning world class races but although he finished third that year — compared to first and second in the two years before — he knew only too well that our machines lacked pace. But, unlike me, he was reluctant to shout his mouth off about action needing to be taken because he valued the security of his factory contract.

Well I couldn't give two hoots. The 250 and 350 Yamahas I rode that season in Britain weren't bad bikes and I wanted the 250 water-cooled Grand Prix one to produce something like the same performance.

But all three class machines would suffer from unreliability; they seemed to have this knack of breaking down so often. So when they again offered a 250 and a 350 for 1973, I knew how pointless it would all be. What I really wanted was a go on the four-cylinder 500cc Yamaha and 750cc machines. Now they could really fly.

They hinted there might be a chance of getting a 500 later on in the season but at the present time, the bikes would be allocated to Jarno Saarinen and Hideo Kanaya who Yamaha were jetting over from Japan to sort out the Grand Prix giants. Big deal! Spares for running a 500 adequately would also be a problem, I was told.

So that did it. My relationship with Yamaha gradually went a little sour, yet early on that season with them they seemed to understand that racers can fall off their bikes or that engines can pack up from time to time. I would have been happy to have stayed with Yamaha. They were a big organisation and they intended to get even bigger. But I needed one thing desperately: machinery good enough to win me a world crown. The 250 seemed as if it would show no improvement and I was being denied the chance to ride a bigger bike. And it was the larger capacity classes I had set my sights on.

So the move to Suzuki resulted. I left Yamaha. They didn't sack me. That should be made crystal clear to the crap-stirrers who relished in my troubles at the time. The Suzuki set-up looked promising and they could provide me with the opportunity to ride a 750 machine. It proved to be the most rewarding decision I had taken.

The three-cylinder 750 Suzuki was, and still could be, a good bit of machinery with enough guts to give a useful account of itself in superbike races. Of course, constant development has meant vast improvement in handling, and speed, in today's model compared to the one I first straddled.

But if any bike was a world-beater then it must be Suzuki's RG500, the four-cylinder beauty that took me to the 500cc classic crown in 1976. For years, MV ruled the roost in the 500cc class, then it was Yamaha's turn to regain the title for Japan. Suzuki became the new kings and I was proud to be associated with them.

Forget the other classes, the 500cc award is the big one; it has always taken pride of place in championship status. The bikes are bigger and more powerful than the rest and I suppose the guys who ride them measure up in the same kind of way. Once I had tasted the delights of racing a 500 bike, the other classes seemed to lose some of their appeal. All the publicity, the glamour and the bulk of prize and start money goes to the 500 boys. One has to assume it's the capacity the public prefer to watch in Grands Prix.

Suzuki had followed their rivals in the international racing game but apart from the occasional high placing here and there, they appeared out of their depth. Their first efforts in the 250 class were a washout. Yet it's hard keeping these Japanese down and a terrific lot of effort was being pumped into their racing set-up. They wanted to outshine Yamaha on the tracks for obvious reasons: Racing success sells road-bikes.

A lot of patient research went into the 500-4 and it is generally reckoned that the former 50cc world champion Ernst Degner was the engineering brains behind the bike's engine lay-out after his defection to Japan and Suzuki from his native East Germany. They say that because the current RG500 engine seems similar in appearance to a couple of 250cc water-cooled MZ twins of the early Sixties — the bike Degner rode.

If this was to be the bike to put Read, Ago and company in the shade, initial results in the Grands Prix suggested that patience was the only requisite before it took over the world.

The bike weighed 319 lb and developed 90 brake horse-power at the beginning of the 1974 campaign and I liked the feel of it. I knew in my own heart that I had at last been provided with super-equipment that would make me number one.

So why did everybody think the machine was a rub-out just because it took so long in winning its first race? That year was one of research and development, a question of getting the bike spot-on and having time to finally uncrease all those niggling problems that always beset a new racing bike. Perserverance. That's what I needed. On a bike that had only gone from the drawing board to the workshop only months before, time was the all-important factor.

When I eventually passed under the chequered flag first at Silverstone in August, 1974, I couldn't resist putting two fingers up to those who maintained the 500-4 was no good or else it was such a beast that it would kill me. That summer's day was a great step forward for me, the bike and the factory.

We hadn't expected to win the world championship series and so Suzuki were not disappointed with my sixth placing in the final analysis that year. I thought I could have done better, but that's me all over; I always set my sights high!

The bike had its troubles, mostly with the drive gear, but testing through the winter by the lads back in Japan seemed to have corrected all those early faults. Whether it would have taken me to the world title is debatable, the pundits echoed after I spent much of 1975 lying flat out on beds or couches.

I know I would have won if it had kept going. Before Daytona, I was brimming over with confidence, I was in the peak of fitness and everything seemed right for me. Events subsequently proved in the summer of '75 that Sheene and the Suzuki 500-4 could see the rest of them off, as shown in Holland and Sweden.

But at the start of '76, Suzuki had constructed what looked like the perfect racing bike. It produced 100 bhp at 11,000 rpm and was capable of reaching over 170 mph. A lot of work had gone into getting my RG500's right at the factory in Hamamatsu and, knowing that Yamaha had largely pulled out of support for the world championship and MV were struggling to sort out their handling difficulties, I knew it was looking good.

My Suzuki was the fastest of any in the early part of 1975 but MV had enough power to match me in the later months and so there was still a feeling that Ago might be a threat on the Italian bike. Read's private Suzukis would also need watching and the development months spent on the Yamaha 500-4's for Cecotto would surely have some effect.

Now it's history. My Suzuki was something special and only once in 1976 Grands Prix did it falter. That was when hot air deflected from the exhausts built up beneath the fuel tank into a kind of 'hot-box' and began to vapourise the petrol which, in turn, led to fuel starvation. Every other time, it went beautifully, as most of us expected although we had to work continuously on the machines. There were, of course, plenty of items replaced, like gearboxes, through the season.

My machines were slightly modified versions of the production RG500 that Suzuki were churning out as standard racers in the middle of '76. In Japan, Suzuki had settled on the square four-cylinder layout and disc inlet valves when designer Makoto Hace was placed in charge of producing the RG500 in 1973. Tests subsequently showed that a bore and stroke of 54mm by 54mm offered better low-speed torque.

Frank Sheene strips down the Suzuki RG500 motor that took his son to a world title. Arthur Sheene looks over his shoulder.

My 1976 racers had a little more horsepower, were slightly lighter and were said to have better handling characteristics when compared to any other 500cc Suzuki available. It was due to Hace's careful and shrewd work that this had been made possible.

Suzuki put in magnesium crankcase castings instead of aluminium, a wider squish band in the heads to give a compression ratio of 8.4 to 1 as opposed to 7.7 to 1 in the standard RG500, and slight modifications to the porting. That gave an extra kick in the power upwards from 6,000 rpm and it peaked at 103 bhp at 11,250 rpm instead of the standard's 100 bhp at 11,000 rpm. With a smaller, lighter magneto and various other bits and bobs changed, around 18 lb was trimmed off the standard bike's weight to make it 297 lb. But, of course, when loaded up with 30 to 1 fuel mixture, it weighed well over 350 lb.

One important aspect of construction that made the machine reliable was the power take-off shaft, made as one piece instead of two and driven by four crankshaft gears. It was the drive gear that caused me so much hardship in '75. Before, the 6 mm bolts that held the two halves of the standard shaft were prone to breakage.

The fine handling of my mounts was mostly due to using gas for the springing in the telescopic front forks in place of coil springs. The gas seemed to help make the forks take the road bumps more easily as it gave the suspension a more progressive movement and could be pumped up to adjust to varying circuits. At the back, wheel travel had been increased by an inch by positioning the bottom lugs for the suspension struts further in along the swinging arm.

It led to better road-holding and so I could slam on the brakes later than most other riders. The rear disc was in cast iron while the double front steel discs were of the normal type. The lightweight calipers on the front discs Suzuki had specially made.

Those refinements gave me around four extra

horsepower to play with compared to the Suzukis Ago, Lansivuori and the like were racing. If people do feel like saying that was why I managed to win five out of six Grands Prix, all I need counter with is that I still had to ride the bike to its maximum. I did just that.

If all my rivals had been aboard the same 'works' RG500 as mine, I'm positive the results would have remained the same. Perhaps one day soon I can prove that I have no need of an advantage, if that's what my 500cc Suzuki was.

Sure my Suzuki was a good bike. There was no doubt it was the best machine I had ever ridden. Suzuki had spent a lot of time getting it right and I had helped them in every way. Remember they started development way back in 1974 on this 500-4.

But now they had got it right and put together a really smart machine, some people reckoned it spoiled the 1976 500cc world championship races because it was so good. Well it wasn't that much better than the other Suzuki 500's. OK, there was more horsepower but it only came in at a certain rev band. In Sweden in the '76 GP where I clinched the title, I was lapping no faster than I did on a standard 500-4 the previous year. In Belgium, both John Williams and John Newbold's bikes were a speed match for mine.

It's a question of being able to ride the thing and that's why I would have been happier winning the championship if all my rivals were on the same type of machine as me. Then there would have been absolutely no disputing I was the best during the season.

My Suzuki had special refinements, I'll admit, and I did find it red hot on braking and bloody quick coming out of corners. But in most other ways, it appeared no better or worse than the other RG500's.

I suppose it's fair to say braking is one of my strong points. I really like to slam on the anchors at the last possible moment. But it's the front discs that are doing all

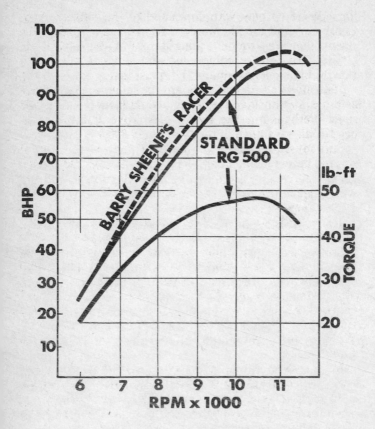

Diagram 1. The solid lines show the power and torque curves of the standard 1976 RG500 Suzuki engine compared to the works power curve (broken line).

the work while the back brake is employed very little. The rear disc is set in a way that, if I want to give it stick at a bend where I might be going too fast, the chances of it locking the wheel are pretty slim.

Suzuki have been good to me. They kept faith with me during the times I lay injured on a hospital bed and they provided me with cracking machinery. There is no reason why I should not be loyal to them in the years to come if their interest in racing continues.

But if Honda did decide to make a full-time comeback to Grand Prix racing with equally good bikes as Suzuki and were offering a lot more money, I wouldn't hesitate in switching factories. It's the money I want to ensure I have security for the rest of my life. I might finish up in a wheelchair in two years' time and have precious little to fall back on.

I doubt very much whether Honda will go GP racing in the near future and I would like to think Suzuki could match any offer of Honda's so it would seem as if I could be a Big S man for quite some time. But one never knows!

I haven't made enough money from racing to retire on, not with my lifestyle the way it is now — and I won't be Britain's first millionaire motorcycle racer for at least another ten years!

But there's far more than cash in this game, as far as I'm concerned. I would say the financial returns from racing come third in the list of priorities every time I wheel my machine out to the grid. First and foremost, it's the right results for all concerned I'm after and then the happiness and satisfaction that goes hand in hand with doing well in front of appreciative audiences. There is no sweeter music to the ears of an entertainer than the rapturous applause of pleased on-lookers.

The cash rewards follow on from the popularity obtained from the sport and so the pounds come well down the list of requirements for much of the time.

Racing motorcycles is the only life I know. It's the only life I want to know. The pleasure I derive from my occupation is enormous and I wouldn't want to change my job for anything.

I once was seen by the Press driving a racing car in France and immediately the rumours were flying around that I might switch to four wheels at some stage. But on that occasion I think I was slightly drunk and only drove the car for a laugh. Unless something really dramatic was to happen, I'm sticking to bikes for my living.

I know Surtees, Hailwood and Ivy turned to four wheels but cars just don't figure in my plans, yet journalists will always pose the question quite frequently. OK, so it's natural to wonder if I'd switch, but some of the things that are printed about me can infuriate me. After I won the world championship a reporter wrote that I could well be going to Honda. That was sheer rubbish. I had never even spoken to Honda. It was just a story made up for gossip purposes. As I have stated, it seems I will continue to be Suzuki-mounted in the 500cc class.

If Suzuki do not come up with a competitive 750cc racer I shall definitely either seriously think about acquiring a Yamaha 750 or else make up a big Suzuki myself as an enlarged version of the 500-4. I would scratch from the Formula 750 Championship and just stick to Britain for 750cc racing.

But, whatever the future brings, I just want to continue to enjoy my racing and keep on winning. The only way I could top my wonderful '76 season would be, I think, to come first in every race I enter.

That will be extremely difficult to achieve but it will be worth watching me try. Certainly, it will only be superior racing motorcycles to mine that will prevent the dream becoming reality. In the past, there hasn't been a rider in the world championships who has outridden me and, looking back over the years, I can truthfully claim that very few of my accidents were caused by a rider error.

That's not meant to sound like a hollow boast. It's fact. I know I'll draw some wry comments for emphasising that point and although I don't believe I'll ever reach the Muhammad Ali level of wild vocal claims, I do reckon I am the best rider around in the world today on whatever kind of machine anyone cares to put me on.

What will Suzuki say? One of Barry's cats and Stephanie McLean's dog find multi-thousand pounds' worth of racing machinery an interesting plaything.

Achievements

1969
125cc British Championship — 2nd

1970
125cc British Championship — 1st
250cc British Championship — 3rd
125cc Spanish Grand Prix — 2nd

1971
125cc World Championship — Second
125cc Austrian Grand Prix — 3rd
125cc Dutch TT — 2nd
125cc Belgian Grand Prix — 1st
125cc East German Grand Prix — 2nd
125cc Czechoslovakian Grand Prix — 3rd
125cc Swedish Grand Prix — 1st
125cc Finnish Grand Prix — 1st
125cc Italian Grand Prix — 3rd
125cc Spanish Grand Prix — 3rd
250cc East German Grand Prix — 6th
50cc Czechoslovakian Grand Prix — 1st
50cc Swedish Grand Prix — 4th
125cc British Championship — 1st
250cc British Championship — 2nd

1972
250cc Austrian Grand Prix — 4th
250cc Spanish Grand Prix — 3rd

1973
Formula 750 Championship — Winner
Formula 750 Championship:
   French round — 1st
   Swedish round — 3rd
   Finnish round — 2nd
   West German round — 4th
   Spanish round — 2nd

MCN Superbike Champion
MCN 'Man of the Year'
King of Brands

1974

500cc World Championship — 6th
500cc French Grand Prix — 2nd
500cc Austrian Grand Prix — 3rd
500cc Czechoslovakian Grand Prix — 4th
Race of the Year, Mallory — 1st
MCN Superbike Championship — 1st
MCN Man of the Year — Runner-up

1975

500cc World Championship — 6th
500cc Dutch TT — 1st
500cc Swedish Grand Prix — 1st
Formula 750 Championship — 2nd
Formula 750 Championship:
    French round - 1st
    British round — 1st
    Swedish round — 1st
Race of the Year, Mallory — 1st
MCN Superbike Championship — 3rd
MCN Man of the Year

1976

500cc World Championship — 1st
500cc French Grand Prix — 1st
500cc Austrian Grand Prix — 1st
500cc Italian Grand Prix — 1st
500cc Dutch TT — 1st
500cc Belgian Grand Prix — 2nd
500cc Swedish Grand Prix — 1st
Race of the Year, Mallory — 2nd